JOSEPH
PRIESTLEY
AND BIRMINGHAM

Malcolm Dick

JOSEPH
PRIESTLEY
AND BIRMINGHAM

Edited by Malcolm Dick

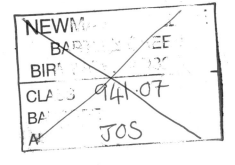

BREWIN BOOKS

First published by
Brewin Books Ltd, 56 Alcester Road,
Studley, Warwickshire B80 7LG in 2005
www.brewinbooks.com

ISBN 1 85858 269 5

A Cataloguing in Publication Record
for this title is available from the British Library

Typeset in Times
Printed in Great Britain by
SupaPrint (Redditch) Limited
www.supaprint.com

CONTENTS

	Acknowledgements	VI
1.	Introduction: Joseph Priestley and Birmingham, *Malcolm Dick*	1
2.	Joseph Priestley: A Timeline, *Malcolm Dick*	5
3.	The Life and Times of Dr Joseph Priestley, *Peter Jones*	7
4.	Gunpowder Joe: Priestley's Religious Radicalism, *Gay Hill*	21
5.	Joseph Priestley: Trail-blazing Experimenter, *Goronwy Tudor Jones*	31
6.	Joseph Priestley and his Influence on Education in Birmingham, *Ruth Watts*	48
7.	Joseph Priestley, the Lunar Society and Anti-slavery, *Malcolm Dick*	65
8.	A Sorry End: The Priestley Riots of 1791, *Peter Leather*	81
9.	Friends Reunited: Dr Priestley and the Russells of Birmingham, *Shena Mason*	90
10.	Joseph Priestley and America, *Malcolm Dick*	105
11.	The Priestley Collection in Birmingham Central Library, *Patrick Baird*	110
12.	Joseph Priestley: A Guide to Further Study, *Malcolm Dick*	111
13.	The Words of Joseph Priestley: Some Examples, *Malcolm Dick*	114
14.	Enlightenment and Dissent: A Poem, *Roi Kwabena*	117
	Contributors	121
	Index	123

ACKNOWLEDGEMENTS

Several people have contributed in important ways to this publication, a special edition of the *Birmingham Historian*. They include the authors who supplied articles promptly and in a form which required little editing.

Four members of the Council of Birmingham and District Local History Association, Patrick Baird, Ivor and Joan Davies and Peter Leather played major roles in creating the project. I am also very grateful to four other members of B&DLHA, Roy Billingham, Kenneth Hughes, James Ruston and Tricia Mason for supplying information or material for publication.

The staff of Birmingham City Archives and the librarians of Local Studies & History in Birmingham Central Library provided many of the sources which are illustrated in this volume. Richard Albutt has efficiently supplied digitised images for the publication. Similarly, several individuals at Birmingham Museums & Art Gallery, especially the staff at Soho House in Handsworth, have also provided images. Without the photography, digitisation and cataloguing for the Revolutionary Players Project which took place between 2002 and 2004, this publication would have been much more difficult to produce. The following individuals contributed to this work: Richard Albutt, Kinson Chan, Kathy Davis, Nabi Heydari, Kate Iles, Chris Sutton, Jo Wong, Andy Willis and Brigitte Winsor. Doreen Hopwood provided a lot of support and guidance during the preparation of the publication.

The Centre for Lifelong Learning at the University of Birmingham has provided a location for the management of the "Joseph Priestley and Birmingham Project". I would like to thank Professor Willie Henderson and his staff, including David King and Marion Cafferkey, for ensuring that the project moved smoothly from conception to birth.

The members of Birmingham and District Local History Association offer their special thanks to the Heritage Lottery Fund for assisting with the funding of the Joseph Priestley and Birmingham Project in general and this publication in particular.

Brewin Books contributed their expertise by producing a first-class publication.

Malcolm Dick

Chapter 1

INTRODUCTION:
JOSEPH PRIESTLEY AND BIRMINGHAM

Malcolm Dick

Joseph Priestley was born in Yorkshire on 13th March 1733 and died on 6th February 1804 in Pennsylvania in the USA. He lived in Birmingham between 1780 and 1791, a period he subsequently described as the happiest time of his life. He became a member of the Lunar Society, a small network of intellectuals, writers, industrialists and humanitarians who travelled across the West Midlands to meet at the time of the full moon. The Lunar Society was never a formally constituted organisation; instead it was a think-tank of philosophers, scientists, writers, inventors and industrialists who discussed the intellectual, scientific and technological activities which were shaping the world at the end of the Eighteenth Century. We know about their work through the letters and books which they wrote and the inventions and manufactured goods that they created. As well as the Rev Dr Priestley, the Lunar men included Matthew Boulton, Erasmus Darwin, Thomas Day, Richard Lovell Edgeworth, Samuel Galton junior, James Keir, William Small, James Watt, Josiah Wedgwood, John Whitehurst and William Withering. In 1791, Priestley was forced to abandon the town he loved following the Priestley Riots, when his house, laboratory and library were destroyed by a mob. Three years later, he found life in Britain to be intolerable and left to spend the rest of his life in the USA [1].

Priestley's contributions are striking. He is probably best-known for his scientific experiments and discoveries with gases and electricity. He identified oxygen as essential for human life and through his work on aerated water Priestley became the father of the fizzy drinks industry! His contributions in other areas, however, were also important. In politics he clarified the distinction between political and civil liberty, believing that the former was a safeguard for the latter, but not essential to it. He defined the purpose of government: to promote the greatest happiness of the greatest number and not to serve the interests of monarchs, landowners or traditional elites in the Established Church. Priestley was a Unitarian, a Christian who did not believe in the divinity of Christ; he was open therefore to the theology of both Judaism and Islam. He could read many languages including Hebrew and Arabic. Priestley's forensic skills, allied to his mastery of Asian and European languages, enabled him to investigate and rewrite the history of Christianity and cut the ground from under the pillars of traditional theology and religious authority. Education, he believed, was central to the well-being of society. This did not mean packing learners with facts and received ideas, but stimulating learning via visual aids and debate and encouraging experimentation and the evaluation of sources. Priestley's advocacy of science, modern history and English Literature revolutionised the curriculum. He encouraged girls and women to learn, think and publish when female education was limited. Women and men, he believed, were equally capable of intellectual development. As a passionate humanitarian, he believed that members of all races and religions required not just toleration, but recognition as intellectual and cultural equals. Priestley was a vehement opponent of slavery and a defender of Jews, Muslims and Catholics when it was fashionable and legally permissible to be prejudiced and discriminatory [2]. Throughout his life he was an advocate of intellectual liberty, believing that unfounded opinions and ignorance could be combated by open-minded enquiry, evidence, and plain speaking.

Plaque to Joseph Priestley on the wall of St. Michael's Catholic Church, Birmingham, formerly Priestley's New Meeting House. Photograph by Roy Billingham.

Priestley was an important contributor to the world in which we live, but he should not be removed from his historical context. He was part of a radical strand of the European Enlightenment that looked optimistically towards the creation of a society which marched inexorably towards human rights and economic progress. This progressive ideology received a severe battering after the Priestley Riots of 1791, the lengthy wars with Revolutionary and Napoleonic France and the domestic political repression from the 1790s until the 1820s. It was not easy to be a liberal in Britain before 1830. Priestley developed his ideas before the French Revolution of 1789 turned from the pursuit of individual liberty towards a military dictatorship and he left England when the British government introduced a range of laws which restricted political protest, the formation of radical organisations such as trade unions and the dissemination of anti-establishment ideas in newspapers and meetings. Priestley was a libertarian, but he opposed poor law relief, which he believed demoralised the poor and advocated severe discipline and punishments for criminals, including the death penalty. Birmingham may have been a dirty and cramped industrial town in the 1780s, but it had a relatively prosperous workforce compared to other industrial centres and it avoided the intense divisions between masters and men which characterised, for example, the Lancashire textile towns [3]. Priestley might be forgiven for not being more critical of the economic and social experience of late Eighteenth-Century Britain.

The New Meeting House, Moor Street and New Meeting Street, Birmingham, where Joseph Priestley preached. The building is now St Michael's Roman Catholic Church. Photograph by Roy Billingham.

Priestley is remembered in Birmingham by a few public monuments. A statue outside the Central Library shows him conducting a scientific experiment and wall plaques identify the site of his former residence in Sparkbrook and his career as a preacher at the New Meeting House, now St Michael's Catholic Church. February 2004 marked the bicentenary of Priestley's death. Priestley was one of Birmingham's most prominent local residents, but there were few local events which commemorated his life and importance in 2004.

The year of his death provided the stimulus behind the "Joseph Priestley and Birmingham Project", which originated within Birmingham and District Local History Association. The Association prepared a bid to the Heritage Lottery Fund to secure £50,000 to help finance a project to draw attention to Priestley and his contributions to Birmingham and the wider world. The bid was successful and work on the project started formally in November 2004. The project aims to celebrate his life and work through publications, exhibitions, signposting the availability of collections, a town trail to draw attention to Birmingham during the time of Joseph Priestley, a DVD of a Priestley scientific experiment and community events. In broad terms it focuses on his contribution to Birmingham and the wider world in areas such as politics, science, education, anti-slavery and racial and religious toleration. The work of the project and material created during its operation will be presented on various websites. These include:

- Revolutionary Players: www.revolutionaryplayers.org.uk
- Birmingham & District Local History Association: www.bdlha.org
- The Centre for Lifelong Learning, University of Birmingham: www.cll.bham.ac.uk

This publication is the first outcome of the project. Several of the contributions were initially presented at a day school "In Praise of Priestley" on Saturday 28th February, organised by the Centre for Lifelong Learning at the University of Birmingham. The features in this publication draw attention to Priestley's life and times, his role as a scientist, promoter of education, radical nonconformist and contributor to anti-slavery. Other articles focus on the Priestley Riots, the Russell family, who also left for the United States of America, and his life and death in Northumberland, Pennsylvania. Contributions at the end of the publication explore the resources which are available to investigate his life and times. The poem by Roi Kwabena, "Enlightenment and Dissent" was written especially to commemorate the 200th anniversary of the death of Joseph Priestley in February 2004.

The "Joseph Priestley and Birmingham Project" provides a different focus to the image of Eighteenth-Century Birmingham as a pioneering industrial town dedicated to metal bashing and making money. Priestley was an important contributor to another aspect of the local experience. Birmingham is a city of diversity, intellectually alive, politically and religiously radical and open to the experiences and influences of other cultures. These characteristics were also present in Eighteenth-Century Birmingham and, if Priestley is relevant to people today, it is because he represents this dimension of contemporary experience.

1   Uglow, Jenny, *The Lunar Men: The Friends who made the Future 1730 – 1810* (London, Faber and Faber, 2002) is a well-researched and readable summary of the Lunar Society and its members.

2   William Hutton, a fellow Unitarian, was not as open as Priestley was to Birmingham's diverse society in the Eighteenth Century. See his comments on local Jews in Hutton, William, *An History of Birmingham* (1781)

3   Hopkins, Eric, *The Rise of the Manufacturing Town: Birmingham and the Industrial Revolution* (Stroud, Sutton Publishing, 1998) provides a summary of economic and social life in Eighteenth-Century Birmingham.

Chapter 2

JOSEPH PRIESTLEY: A TIMELINE

Malcolm Dick

1733. 13th March 1733, Joseph Priestley was born near Leeds, Yorkshire into a family of cloth workers and dressers. He was raised as a nonconformist and studied at Batley Grammar School.

1752. Priestley entered the Dissenting Academy at Daventry to begin theological training where he also studied philosophy, mathematics, history and science. He learned Latin, Greek, Hebrew, French, German, Italian, Arabic and other languages.

1755. He began his career as a minister in Needham Market, Suffolk.

1758. Priestley moved to Nantwich, Cheshire, as minister to another congregation.

1761. Priestley joined the teaching staff at Warrington Academy, where he lectured in English, Latin and History and wrote his *Essay on Government* (1768). It argued that the purpose of government should be to promote the "greatest happiness of the greatest number". He met Benjamin Franklin who encouraged him to write *The History and Present State of Electricity* (1767).

1762. Priestley was ordained as a minister and married Mary Wilkinson, the daughter of Isaac Wilkinson, the ironmaster and brother of John "iron-mad" Wilkinson.

1767. He left Warrington, becoming a minister in Leeds. Here he resumed his theological studies and experimented with acids and gases. His investigations contributed to the later emergence of the fizzy drinks industry and the discovery of nitric oxide, nitrous oxide and nitrogen oxide.

1772. Priestley moved to Bowood House in Wiltshire. Financed by its owner, Lord Shelburne, Priestley was able to publish his philosophical studies and scientific experiments. He isolated "dephlogisticated air" or oxygen and investigated other gases and electricity. He acquired a European reputation for his contributions to knowledge.

1780. Priestley left Wiltshire and moved to Birmingham, settling at Fair Hill. He became a Unitarian minister, met with other members of the Lunar Society and created a laboratory for his experiments. He wrote on matters relating to religious liberty, the reduction of poverty and anti-slavery. He became nationally famous for his campaign to repeal The Test and Corporation Acts which restricted the rights of nonconformists compared to Anglicans. Priestley became the subject of criticism and ridicule from cartoonists.

1791. Priestley defended the French Revolution against the critical writings of Edmund Burke. During the anti-radical "Priestley Riots" his house, library and laboratory were destroyed. He was forced to leave Birmingham.

1794. He left England for the USA where he settled in Northumberland, Pennsylvania.

1804. 6th February 2004, Joseph Priestley died.

Print of Joseph Priestley aged 30 from a photograph of a portrait. Local Studies and History, Birmingham Central Library.

Chapter 3

THE LIFE AND TIMES OF DR JOSEPH PRIESTLEY

P. M. Jones

Two hundred years ago, on 6th February 1804, Joseph Priestley Doctor of Laws, minister of religion, theologian, scientist and political reformer, passed away. Thomas Cooper who was with him at the end wrote that same day to a mutual acquaintance: "Your old friend Dr Priestley died this morning without pain at 11 o'clock. He would have been 71 had he lived till the 24th of next month. He continued composed and cheerful to the end. He had been apprised of his approaching dissolution for some days" [1]. Although he had been ill and in obvious decline since the previous November, Priestley had managed to keep on working in short bouts. And it was richly characteristic of the man that he should allow himself to die that morning only after having corrected some pamphlets which he had requested his son Joseph to bring to his bedside – religious pamphlets.

Print of Joseph Priestley. Priestley Collection by Samuel Timmins, Birmingham City Archives.

We mark Priestley's passing by exploring the facets of a remarkably full and rewarding life. Yet it has to be acknowledged that he died a largely forgotten man. He died separated from his homeland in a remote and tiny settlement in the backwoods of Pennsylvania, America. He died separated from his scientific colleagues in Europe and almost completely out of touch with the experimental work in electrostatics and chemistry which he had done so much to advance in the early part of his career. He died, as he had lived, a religious outsider. And he died an unrepentant political exile whose enthusiasm for the actions of the French revolutionaries proved almost as distasteful to the Americans as it had to his fellow Englishmen.

At the religious service held to honour his memory at the Unitarian New Meeting Church in Birmingham in February 2004, the presiding minister described Priestley as a 'man of candour', a description that I would not dissent from – even if Priestley was capable of deceiving himself on occasions. He *was* a transparent man, a man who had no need of disguises, who never obfuscated, who was never slow to admit to a change of opinion. For a historian such as myself his life is relatively easy to follow, for much of it was spent in the public domain – under public scrutiny – and Priestley, as I have said, was not a man to wear masks.

It is true that the sources allowing us to reconstruct his life are now scattered; that the papers relating to the early and middle periods of his life were nearly all lost during the Birmingham riots of 1791; that Mrs Priestley had a tiresome habit of burning her own incoming correspondence; and that many of Priestley's contemporaries either had their own correspondence destroyed in fires, or posthumously destroyed by overly solicitous relatives. Shortly before his death Priestley, too, disposed of some of his incoming correspondence, which is a shame. But much remains – not least the twenty-five volumes of his collected works. And as a social historian whose principal occupation up to now has been to coax inarticulate country dwellers to speak, I am more impressed by what we know, or can find out about Joseph Priestley than by what remains inaccessible, or concealed from view.

My paper will provide an overview of Priestley's career. The aim is to provide a frame of reference.

* * * * *

Joseph Priestley was born into a family of woollen cloth workers and dressers in the West Riding of Yorkshire, just outside Leeds, in 1733. He came from a modest but comfortable craft background. However the family was disrupted early on by the death of his mother, which resulted in Joseph and his five siblings being raised by an aunt and uncle who were markedly better off. His adoptive parents were Calvinists, albeit fairly liberal-minded Calvinists, and they would have a powerful influence on his subsequent development. His formal schooling seems to have been spasmodic and to have consisted mainly of stints at Batley grammar school and home instruction from visiting Presbyterian ministers. In this respect his early years bear a resemblance to those of James Watt, the steam engine pioneer and future Lunar associate. Watt had a rather similar Calvinist upbringing leavened with attendance at the grammar school in Greenock. Watt, also, was an experimenter and tinkerer from an early age.

Birthplace of Joseph Priestley, Fieldhead, Leeds, Yorkshire. Birmingham City Archives, Priestley Collection by Samuel Timmins.

Priestley's aunt would have liked him to become an orthodox Calvinist minister, and with this aim in mind he was sent to Daventry Academy in 1752. Dissenters, that is to say non-Anglicans, were largely excluded from the ancient English universities at the time, and the academies acted as dissenter universities to all intents and purposes. At Daventry Priestley would build up and consolidate his education. He also received a rigorous training in the skills of free enquiry that would become his stock-in-trade for the rest of his life.

It is worth asking what species of Christian Priestley was becoming while undergoing training. Loosely speaking he was a dissenter of course: he dissented from the official doctrines of the established church, the Church of England. But this is not to say very much in an environment of religious pluralism such as that prevailing in England in the early decades of the Eighteenth Century. When the French *philosophe* Voltaire visited our shores in the 1720s, he marvelled at a country that had only one sauce but numerous religious denominations. There was "Old Dissent" and "New Dissent": Presbyterians and Quakers; Baptists and Independents. These sects, it is important to remember, tended to disagree with one another almost as much as they disagreed with the established church. Moreover, Anglicanism was scarcely monolithic: it was riven by the Arian controversy during the early part of the Century, and by Methodism during the latter part.

The Academy at Daventry, Northamptonshire, known as Doddridge Academy, which Priestley attended between 1752 and 1755. Photograph by Roy Billingham.

While at Daventry, the evidence suggests that Priestley moved in the direction of Arianism; that is to say towards a point of view that did not deny the divinity of Christ even though it questioned the Trinity insofar as Arians placed God the Father above and beyond the Son and the Holy Spirit. Later on in life Priestley would write that he was an Arian until 1767 when he took up the post of minister to Mill Hill chapel in Leeds. Much later still, in 1801, he would condemn the "folly" [2] of Arianism in no uncertain terms. But Unitarianism – his final religious resting place – scarcely existed as a belief system in 1767, whereas by 1801 it was fully fledged. Unitarianism, or "One-goddism" [3], as the poet Samuel Taylor Coleridge summarised it somewhat dismissively, *did* reject the divinity of Christ and therefore completely undermined the doctrine of the Trinity. This placed Priestley beyond the Pale, not just in terms of the established church but in the eyes of many dissenter congregations as well. It meant that he could be depicted as an enemy of Christianity. It was the principal cause of the travails and setbacks he faced during his life.

After Daventry, Joseph Priestley held several posts in quick succession. Between 1755 and 1758 he ministered to a small Presbyterian congregation in Needham Market, Suffolk; then he moved on to a post at Nantwich in Cheshire. In 1761 he was appointed tutor in languages and literature at the recently established Warrington Academy, and it was here that he first discovered his talent as a teacher and a populariser. The post also gave him more time and the financial wherewithal to indulge his love of natural philosophy, as experimental science was then known. His first scientific publication, *The History and Present State of Electricity* (1767), dates from this period, and it earned him election to the Royal Society. He also got married, taking Mary, sister of the famous ironmasters John and William Wilkinson, as his bride.

The 1760s and 1770s were the most enduringly productive decades of Joseph Priestley's life. During these years he refined and stabilised his religious beliefs; he discovered his talent as a communicator; and, of course, he started to acquire a formidable reputation as an experimental scientist. Between 1767 and 1774 he made fundamental discoveries in the field of electrostatics and gaseous chemistry, with the result that his reputation and network of correspondents spread across the whole of Europe. He also discovered that he possessed a ready pen and began to develop the pamphlet mode of discourse and polemic that would become his hallmark.

The Earl of Shelburne, Priestley's patron from 1772 to 1780.
Birmingham City Archives, Priestley Collection by Samuel Timmins.

Leisure, patrons and financial resources were the keys to his success in these years, I think. After a further stint as a pastor ministering to the large congregation of Mill Hill chapel in Leeds (1767-1773), he had entered the service of the Earl of Shelburne in the role of librarian. The position paid £250.00 per annum and came with a house and access to a fine library and laboratory. It also provided an entrée to the highest society in the land, notwithstanding Priestley's religious opinions which many found repugnant. Shelburne also took him on the continental Grand Tour and introduced him to some of the central figures of the European Enlightenment. He met *philosophes* (not to mention archbishops and bishops) who did not believe in God; men who were equally taken aback to discover that he, Priestley, did. Science and religion – or maybe we should say religion as revealed by the Roman Catholic church – did not make for easy bed fellows on the continent in these decades. However for Priestley there was no tension between his religion and his experimental activities – quite the opposite in fact. If we lose sight of the point that his science served his religion, and not *vice versa*, we risk gravely misunderstanding the man.

Among the numerous academicians whom Priestley met in Paris in 1774 was Antoine Lavoisier (1743-1794) whose work would place chemistry on entirely new theoretical foundations by the end of the Century. Sadly, most of the Priestley–Lavoisier correspondence was lost during the Birmingham riots of 1791. I think that only one letter survives; but we do know that their meeting in the autumn of 1774 had momentous consequences for Priestley gave Lavoisier a verbal account of how he had recently stumbled upon a new gas which he had labelled "dephlogisticated air" since it supported combustion so much better than ordinary air. With his vastly expensive, high-precision apparatus Lavoisier quickly replicated Priestley's experiments and in due course re-labelled the newly isolated gas "oxygène".

During these years Priestley also made durable friendships in the world of non-conformity, and it is from the surviving correspondence with men like Dr Richard Price and the Revd Theophilus Lindsey (founding father of Unitarianism) that we really get the measure of our man. Above all, we get a sense of the centrality of his religious beliefs and of his unending quest to uncover the authentic voice of scriptural authority by stripping away all man-made doctrinal accretions.

Antoine Lavoisier, the French chemist, whom Priestley met in 1774. Birmingham City Archives, Priestley Collection by Samuel Timmins.

His growing self-confidence and vigour as both a religious and a political controversialist was probably what brought the Shelburne phase of his career to an end. In 1780 the earl and his companion-librarian parted company, an event which launched Joseph Priestley into the second and more sombre – one might almost say more destructive – phase of his life. That year he arrived in Birmingham and took up the post of minister to the New Meeting, one of the town's Presbyterian congregations.

Birmingham in the Eighteenth Century was an extraordinarily dynamic and inventive place. Little more than a large industrial village at the start of the Century, it was expanding at a faster rate than any other centre of population in England with the possible exception of Sheffield. By the end of the third quarter of the Century it had become the third largest town in England and Wales (after London and Bristol). By the Century's end it boasted nearly 74,000 inhabitants, although the population peak may have occurred a decade earlier. It was a manufacturing town, of course; indeed 'the first manufacturing town in the world' according to the travel writer Arthur Young [4]. Utilitarian hardware was its stock-in-trade, but a switch to ornamental metal goods was under way – buttons, buckles, watch chains, snuff boxes, small brass objects and so forth – much of which was produced for export markets.

Like all new centres of population at this time, it was a notably free and easy place in which to get work and make, or lose, money. There was no corporation or town council, no guilds and no entrenched elite. The religious affiliations of the bulk of the population were certainly Anglican, but there also existed a dissenting minority which happened to include many of the town's richer inhabitants. To be precise, mid-Century Birmingham boasted two long-established Presbyterian or Calvinist communities, a small Quaker community

Reverend Theophilus Lindsay, the founder of Unitarianism. Birmingham City Archives, Priestley Collection by Samuel Timmins.

and a more recently established congregation of Baptists. On the whole, and by the standards of other Eighteenth-Century provincial towns, this large concentration of labouring people rubbed along fairly well. Unrest triggered by soaring food prices occurred from time to time; there had been serious civil disturbances in 1715, and there would be more in 1791 and in 1839. Between times, however, rich and poor and dissenters and churchmen co-existed reasonably amicably. This, then, was the situation when Dr Joseph Priestley arrived and took over the New Meeting – the more liberal of the two Presbyterian congregations – in October 1780.

If relations between the various communities making up the town were not habitually conflictual, whether in 1780 or even 1785, it becomes something of a challenge to explain how the atmosphere which gave rise to the riots of 1791 came into being. I think the answer has to be sought first and foremost at the national, even the international level. Nevertheless, Priestley himself cannot escape a share of the responsibility for what happened in 1791. If Joseph Priestley had not moved to Birmingham in 1780, is it likely that the riots would have occurred notwithstanding? I think not.

The national-level factor that poisoned the atmosphere of civic cooperation in the town after 1785 was undoubtedly the dissenter campaign for the repeal of the

*Westley's East Prospect of Birmingham, published about 1730, from Dent, R K, Old and
New Birmingham (Birmingham, Houghton and Hammond, 1880).*

Test and Corporation Acts. This was the legislation dating mostly from the
Seventeenth Century which served to remind dissenters that they had once been
actively persecuted minorities. The impediments to office holding by dissenters had
mostly been overcome by the second half of the Eighteenth Century, it is true, but
the presence of this legislation on the statute book continued to cause huge symbolic
and some practical offence. Motions for repeal were moved in the House of
Commons in 1787, in 1789 and in 1790, but they all failed (that of May 1789 by
only 20 votes). Dissenters in Birmingham, in common with their co-religionaries in
other big towns, were extremely active in this repeal movement, and there can be
little doubt that the campaign stirred up deep-seated sectarian animosities.

What about the international factor intruding upon the surface calm of English
domestic politics? The irritant here was the outbreak of the French Revolution in 1789,
and it is important to remember that the occasion for the rioting in 1791 was the
holding of a celebratory dinner on 14th July to mark the second anniversary of the fall
of the Bastille. Who were the most conspicuous and voluble supporters of the French
revolutionaries in towns like Birmingham? They were the dissenters. After 1789 such
men would draw a neat, if not altogether convincing, parallel between the struggle of
the French against Bourbon absolutism and their own struggle against the Hanoverian
state. Dissenters were not the only group to welcome the French Revolution, of course.
The spectacle of political reform across the Channel enthused many adherents of the
established church also. However, the link between Dissent and French-style *liberté*
endured, whereas the inclination of other groups to use the example of France for
domestic purposes proved short-lived.

A third element can be identified in this volatile admixture of political liberty and dissenting religion: the rapidly expanding science of gaseous chemistry. Who, we must ask, were the prophets of the new chemistry? They were French men like Lavoisier, Berthollet, Guyton de Morveau and Fourcroy. And who was perceived to be their most outspoken English interlocutor? Dr Joseph Priestley. For defenders of the British Constitution, such as Edmund Burke, the connection was unmistakable. In his famously lyrical diatribe against the French revolutionaries, *Reflections on the Revolution in France* (1790), he likened liberty to a "wild *gas*" [5] – no accidental choice of metaphor.

The New Meeting House, in William Hutton, An History of Birmingham, (1781 edition).

What of Priestley's personal responsibility in all of this? He had a facile pen as I have already pointed out, and was scarcely a man to recoil from controversy. When attacked he always counter-attacked, often to the point of recklessness. He goaded his religious and political opponents and was goaded by them in return. So much so that engaging Dr Priestley in controversy became a recognised route for promotion with the Church of England. A year or so after the riots William Hutton, Birmingham's first historian, remarked wryly that Priestley "had already made two bishops; and there were still several heads which wanted mitres" [6]. One of these was Spencer Madan, rector of St Philip's, who from 1787 became Priestley's principal local adversary among the churchmen. In 1792 he was rewarded for his services with the bishopric of Bristol. Joseph Priestley's taste for colourful and prophetic utterances, a characteristic of the Unitarians, could also get him into trouble. In a sermon preached in 1785 he used a metaphor which would prove a real hostage to fortune when he likened the efforts of Rational Dissent to gunpowder laid "grain by grain under the old building of error and superstition, which a single spark may hereafter inflame, so as to produce an instantaneous explosion" [7]. This is the origin of the nickname "Gunpowder Joe" which, in the very different political climate of the 1790s, would replace the more respectful "Proteus Priestley".

* * * * *

Our hero was sitting at home in Sparkbrook playing backgammon with his wife on the evening of 14th July 1791 when the news arrived that rioters from Birmingham were heading his way. The dissenter meeting houses appear to have been the main targets of the mob, including the Quaker premises in Bull Street. Priestley's own house at Fairhill was ransacked and set alight, as were the properties of more than twenty other prominent citizens – most of them dissenters. Priestley fled to London, to be joined shortly thereafter by his family. He would never again set foot in Birmingham. Little or nothing of any consequence was saved from the conflagration at Fairhill: experimental apparatus, books, hand-written sermons, diaries, papers and letter correspondence were either consumed by the flames or looted by the crowd. An acquaintance who mingled with the rioters as they demolished his house reported that "the road for half a mile of my approach was strewn with your books, the mob were carrying others away, and there were not above twelve octavoes on the shelves when I entered the room, the floor of which was totally covered, two or three inches deep, with torn leaves, chiefly manuscript" [8].

It was a personal tragedy, a tragedy for the Birmingham dissenter community, and, more generally, a tragedy for the spirit of free enquiry all rolled into one. Moreover, the Birmingham riots had far reaching repercussions across the nation for they turned the tide of opinion against would-be reformers of all persuasions – religious, political and scientific. While French chemists hastened to condole and commiserate, the Royal Society remained silent. Even some of Priestley's friends in the Lunar Society adopted a pained stance, implying in their demeanour that he had, in part, been the author of his own misfortunes. But at least Mrs Priestley did not lose her sense of humour. In a letter to Mrs Barbauld she thanked heaven that she had burned all of her personal correspondence before it could be burned, observing furthermore that it was an ill wind that blew nobody any good. To the astonishment and irritation of the town's medical practitioners, all their nervous patients and hypochondriacs had been cured by the drama!

The Priestley family did not decide to emigrate immediately. Joseph senior tried to rebuild his life in London with the financial help of friends and his brother-in-law John Wilkinson. He also drew on his spiritual reserves and a huge fund of biblical knowledge which allowed him to construe the workings of Providence and to find solace in even the most unpromising of situations. He even resumed his experiments, whilst admitting in a revealing letter, that social contact and context count for everything in matters relating to scientific endeavour. "There are few things I regret [more] in consequence of my removal from Birmingham", he informed his Lunar friends, "than the loss of your society. It both encouraged and enlightened me, so that what I did there of a philosophical kind ought in justice to be attributed almost as much to you as to myself" [9].

However, he was now in the grip of powerful forces over which he had little or no control. For one thing there was a real risk that the mob might pay him a repeat visit in his new abode. As the anniversary of the riots came around, his Hackney neighbours were in daily expectation of something of the sort apparently. Then there was the problem of his sons, Joseph, William and Harry, who needed to make their way in the world and yet found all doors closed to them. Finally there was the deteriorating international situation: as the example of France became ever more blood stained the winds of "liberty" began to escape the sails of the reformers and to fill those of the conservatives instead. In February 1793 war broke out between Britain and France. This development placed men like Priestley and his son William in an awkward situation. In common with Tom Paine, author of *Rights of Man* (1791), they had accepted an offer of French citizenship in a symbolic gesture of solidarity with the French nation. Yet in the new context of armed hostilities, such gestures could easily be misunderstood. Fearing arrest, Paine left for France in the autumn of 1792 and Priestley briefly considered removing himself from the scene in similar fashion.

Little persuading was needed to convince him that America offered the better prospect, however. First his sons went out in order to reconnoitre the landscape both physically and figuratively. It had been suggested that intending English refugees should found a model community, either in Ohio or on the Susquehanna River in Pennsylvania. "Old Priestley", as he was now known, only set sail with his wife from the Thames on 7th April 1794. The government's law officers did not prevent them from leaving, but few lamented their departure either. For safety their vessel, the *Hope*, joined a convoy of merchantmen in the Channel and, after a lengthy crossing, reached the shores of America early in June.

Priestley found it difficult to write whilst at sea. Instead he took the opportunity to re-read the Greek Testament and the Hebrew Bible as far as the first Book of Samuel. There were only eight or nine other cabin passengers, but the steerage was packed with men and their families going into exile. During the voyage he provided religious services for all and sundry, while noting that there was more religion in steerage than in the cabin quarters. However, the majority of the below- deck passengers were Calvinists. Re-united with his sons, Priestley spent the last ten years of his life in America. He would die there, along with his youngest son and his wife Mary. Sarah, his married daughter who was better known as Sally, had not made the journey and would predecease him in England.

Did America turn out to be the Promised Land? I think not. The infant United States was going through its own political turmoils at this juncture, and refugees such as Priestley who might have been involved in sedition or even conspiracy were scarcely welcomed with open arms, particularly those who, in addition, attracted suspicion on religious grounds. Moreover the young republic was not on good diplomatic terms with either Britain or France during these years, and there was a constant danger that it would be sucked into the continental European war. While his sons settled down to rustic pursuits, Priestley felt marooned. He was living in a modest settlement five days journey from Philadelphia; just getting the mail and parcels of books from Philadelphia to Northumberland was quite an undertaking. As for chemical apparatus, that was another matter altogether.

But Philadelphia, too, was cut off for long periods, particularly during the winter time. When living in Birmingham, Priestley had been accustomed to receiving communications from Paris in four days, but in April 1796 he complained to the Revd Lindsey that no news had reached Philadelphia from Europe for seventy-five days. Not surprisingly, he entertained near constant thoughts of returning to Europe, whether to England or to France. However, he was getting old and frail, and for as long as the continental war endured the Atlantic sea passage remained unsafe for passengers travelling on American vessels.

What he really wanted to do was to preach and to carry out experiments. Yet neither was really feasible in his adoptive land. There was no chapel or congregation at Northumberland, and few were keen to lend him a pulpit in Philadelphia. He was, after all, a denier of the Trinity, albeit a very learned and eminent one. In January 1798 he confided in a letter to John Hurford Stone in Paris that "I am subject to more coarse abuse, as a friend of France, than I ever was in England" [10]. As the struggle between the Federalists and the Jeffersonian democrats reached fever pitch, Priestley found himself condemned on two counts: a dangerous republican and one with unorthodox religious views to boot!

On the science front Priestley did eventually manage, by 1797, to set up a reasonably well equipped laboratory. And he would make the most of the principal natural advantage of his new situation, namely sunlight to power his magnifying glass. But he was completely out of the swim as far as experimentation was concerned. There existed no network of fellow practitioners such as the Lunar Society, and if we can judge from the chance survival of letters covering this period, his scientific correspondence was desultory at best. As an adherent to the phlogiston doctrine in chemistry, he was something of a relic in any case. Few if any of his erstwhile collaborators in Europe still clung to the belief in the existence of phlogiston. His main intellectual pastime during the final years seems rather to have been religious introspection: the re-examining and re-working of the articles of his faith. Also biblical exegesis, in an attempt to match up the prophesies contained in the Books of Daniel, Kings and Revelation with the events unfolding in the world about him.

* * * * *

What final judgement should we pass on Dr Joseph Priestley? He has been depicted as a stern man, a man who took the view that it was preferable that the

Joseph Priestley House, Northumberland, Pennsylvania, from the south-east showing Priestley's laboratory. Birmingham City Archives. Priestley Collection by Samuel Timmins.

innocent should suffer than the guilty escape. It is true that he was an uncompromising believer in social discipline and opposed to the systematic provision of poor law relief. Yet sterness is not the description I would choose in order to characterise the man. Austere, perhaps, but not stern. His greatest talents, it seems to me, lay in the field of communication, teaching and pastoral care. He never tired in the role of propagator of knowledge – accessible knowledge that could be internalised by all and sundry of whatever social station. Nothing grieved him more than to see the conservative reaction in 1790s England clamping down on even the most anodyne outlets for knowledge. In a letter written just a few months before his exodus, he contrasted the progress being made by the French in setting up a national system of education with the situation in England where even Sunday schools "begin to be reprobated as making the people too knowing" [11].

In matters to do with legislation and institutional reform, there is a pleasing lack of cant about the man. Even though he believed Roman Catholics to be profoundly misguided, they too, he insisted, should enjoy the fruits of emancipation. Jews likewise. But he could be reckless, even irresponsible, in his own political cause. Priestley's protestations that he was uninvolved in the preparations for the notorious dinner of 14th July 1791 in Birmingham scarcely ring true. And much later, while in Pennsylvania, his prowess as a controversialist led him astray once again. Despite insisting that he was a stranger in a foreign land, he allowed himself to be drawn into party politics. This episode, too, nearly ended in expulsion.

In matters scientific and more especially chemical, Priestley never disguised the fact that he lacked formal training. In answer to the suggestion that he should take up a lectureship in Philadelphia, he admitted to Revd Lindsey that "I never gave much attention to the common routine of it [chemistry] and know little of the common practices" [12]. Yet the accusation that he was a dabbler is misplaced because nearly all of the natural philosophers of his generation were eclectic experimenters. As for the casual disregard of routine, it may actually help us to understand how he was able to make fundamental discoveries.

If anyone was an exception to the rule in terms of methodology, it appears to have been Lavoisier, not Priestley. By making explicit their theoretical assumptions, the French academicians were signalling that the Baconian tradition of observation and experiment was no longer sufficient on its own. Knowledge – chemical knowledge – was accumulating rapidly in the second half of the Eighteenth Century and it needed new techniques if it was to be properly ordered. Priestley was dubious, if only for the reason that the new theoretically-informed and quantitatively-driven chemistry was actually harder for lay people to grasp, particularly when it was expressed in a kind of algebraic jargon.

In the end, though, the scientific world would agree with Lavoisier, and Dr Joseph Priestley, the talented practitioner and teacher, was shunted into one of History's sidings. This is where he remains. But in the city of Birmingham, at least, we are making amends for the treatment meted out to him by our forebears.

Notes

1 Birmingham Central Library, Archives of the Church of the Messiah 238, T. Cooper to J. Woodhouse, 6th February 1804.

2 J. Priestley to T. Lindsey, 2nd October 1801 *in* J. T. Rutt, *Life and Correspondence of Joseph Priestley* (2 vols., London, 1831-32), ii, p. 469.

3 See A. D. Orange, *Joseph Priestley 1733-1804* (Aylesbury, 1974), p. 23.

4 See E. Hopkins, *The Rise of the Manufacturing Town: Birmingham and the Industrial Revolution* (Guildford, 1998), p. xiii.

5 E. Burke, *Reflections on the Revolution in France* (Penguin, 1973), p. 90.

6 See Rutt, *Life and Correspondence*, ii, p.188.

7 J. Money, *Experience and Identity: Birmingham and the West Midlands, 1760-1800* (Manchester, 1977), p. 219.

8 See Rutt, *Life and Correspondence*, ii, p. 116 note.

9 *Ibid.*, ii, p. 209.

10 *Ibid.*, ii, p. 393.

11 *Ibid.*, ii, pp. 207-8.

12 *Ibid.*, ii, p. 306.

Chapter 4

GUNPOWDER JOE:
PRIESTLEY'S RELIGIOUS RADICALISM

Gay Hill

Joseph Priestley's importance as a scientist, theologian, philosopher and political theorist has long been recognised. John Ruskin Clark called him a "comet in the system" [1] but a meteor might be a more apt description, a brilliant or dazzling shooting star, which was destined to be short-lived. In Priestley's case this was bound to happen, given the opposition and even resentment that his natural brilliance attracted. Furthermore, Priestley was no stranger to controversy and, indeed, it could even be argued that he courted and relished controversy, despite his protestations of innocence: "Besides, my controversial writings bear but a small proportion to the rest of my publications" [2].

Priestley was undoubtedly loved by many of his contemporaries as well as hated by his opponents. We have many surviving contemporary opinions of him but most of these were from fellow Unitarians or other dissenters. Mary Anne Schimmelpenninck, daughter of the Birmingham Quaker, Samuel Galton, and fellow Lunar Society member, described him as: "A man of admirable simplicity, gentleness and kindness of heart, united with great acuteness of intellect...and utterly far as I am removed from a belief in the sufficiency of Dr Priestley's theological creed, I cannot but here record this evidence of the eternal power of any portion of the truth held in its vitality" [3].

Catherine Hutton, daughter of William Hutton who was a fellow sufferer in the 1791 Riots, was a devoted member of Priestley's congregation. She described him as "fervent, though not intemperate" [4]. Possibly her love and sympathy for him coloured her opinion. Even the greatest of Priestley's admirers could hardly describe his religious and political views as not intemperate. A more balanced view of Priestley came from Catherine's father, who, although having good reason to resent Priestley for being the cause of the riots in which he also suffered greatly, concluded: "However just might have been Dr Priestley's sentiments, yet had he not had promulgated them on one side, and party violence opposed them on the other, perhaps the peace of my life had never been wrecked in the terrible tempest of ninety-one" [5]. Even Catherine later agreed with her father that Priestley was not such an innocent victim of the riots [6].

After the 1791 riots, Priestley was quick to proclaim his innocence. He wrote: "the only sufferers were that very description of men against whom the popular resentment had been excited several years before, viz. the Unitarian Dissenters in general, and myself in particular, whether we were at the dinner, or concerned in promoting it, or not... Of the principal sufferers...only three were at the dinner, and their houses were the last that were destroyed" [7]. Immediately before leaving for America in 1794 Priestley referred to: "the great odium that I have incurred; the charge of sedition, or of my being an enemy of the constitution or peace of my country" [8].

Portrait of Joseph Priestley. Priestley Collection by Samuel Timmins, Birmingham City Archives.

As Martin Smith quite rightly points out, although Priestley could indeed claim that he had only been defending himself against his detractors, it should be remembered that he had many axes to grind [9]. Priestley denied all interest in what could be termed high politics, that is, party politics [10], but was more interested in what he called freedom. He distinguished between two different kinds of liberty, civil and political, in his "Essays on the First Principles of Government" [11]. In 1793, he wrote to the Morning Chronicle: "I am not, nor ever was, a member of any political society whatever, nor did I ever sign any paper originating with any of them."

Taken at face value, this denial appears to be unequivocal. However, he apparently pressurised both Matthew Boulton and James Watt, fellow members of the Lunar Society, to join him as members of the Warwickshire Constitutional Society only two weeks before the riots of 1791 [12]. Although, strictly speaking, this denial was true, as no agreement was actually signed, it would appear that he was being deliberately economical with the truth.

Political tensions in England were much greater after the French Revolution started in 1789. Many within the English Establishment saw the revolution as a dangerous precedent and were particularly uneasy, because of the comparisons that could be drawn with the execution of Charles I in the Seventeenth Century. Many Dissenters, including Priestley, applauded events in France, not necessarily because they hoped for the overthrow of the monarchy in England. Much of Priestley's pamphlet war with Spencer Madan in 1790 was taken up with Priestley's protestations, on behalf of Presbyterians in general, of their loyalty to the present system, while at the same time pressing for both political and religious reforms [13].

It is curious that Priestley's belief in civil liberty did not extend to his opinions on poor law relief, of which he was a stern opponent, nor to his belief in stern social discipline. He was a strong believer in capital punishment, solitary confinement and meagre diets as part of vigorous punishment for criminals [14]. Again, these opinions naturally attracted the opposition and even hatred of the

James Watt, one of the Priestley's colleagues in the Lunar Society. Priestley tried to persuade Watt to join the Warwickshire Constitutional Society in 1791. Image from Local Studies and History, Birmingham Central Library.

poorer classes, once they had been made aware of Priestley's views. The pamphlets aimed against Priestley and attributed to one John Nott, although there is no proof that Nott actually existed, were quite clearly written to appeal to the artisan classes, who were unlikely to have ever read Priestley's writings or heard any of his sermons: "If you ben't melancholy mad, as I guess you to be, what makes you rave so much about gunpowder...Why you'd be frightened out of your senses" [15].

In stark contrast to his firm beliefs in strict social discipline, Priestley was a strong believer in complete freedom of worship. This was extended to its logical conclusion, including Roman Catholics and even non-Christians. He was one of the few non-conformist supporters of the Catholic Relief Act of 1791, which introduced formal toleration of Catholic worship and schools [16]. While these views found favour with Roman Catholics, who probably mistrusted Priestley's motives, they were anathema to many of his fellow Dissenters.

One fellow Dissenter who disliked and mistrusted Priestley was John Wesley. He declared Priestley "one of the most dangerous enemies of Christianity" [17]. Possibly Wesley saw Priestley as a threat to his particular brand of enthusiastic Christianity, Methodism, which appealed more to the lower classes. There was even a popular Methodist hymn lampooning Priestley: "Stretch out thy hands, thou Triune God:/ The Unitarian fiend expel/ And chase his doctrine back to hell" [18]. Wesley need not have worried. The feelings were entirely mutual. Priestley disliked all forms of enthusiasm in religion, and was unlikely to want to appeal to the lower classes in this way. He retaliated in his anonymous tract, *Appeal to the Professors of Christianity* [19].

In his religious views Priestley attracted most opposition and almost hatred from the Established Church, the Church of England. Some of his most vociferous opponents were churchmen. William Hutton even cynically claimed that they could make their names from attacking Priestley. "To dispute with the doctor was deemed the road to preferment. He had already made two bishops, and there were still several heads, which wanted mitres, and others who cast

Portrait of John Wesley struck off by electricity by Joseph Priestley. Birmingham City Archives, Priestley Collection by Samuel Timmins.

a more humble eye upon tithes and glebe lands" [20]. Hutton had a point; Priestley was following in the footsteps of the 17th Quakers by threatening the livelihoods of Anglican churchmen. Paul Langford called Priestley the high priest of rational dissent [21], which, as Roy Porter has explained, was the natural conclusion of "the searchlight of reason and standard of debate [22]". Despite the illusion of religious toleration, after the misnamed Toleration Act of 1689, the provisions of the Test and Corporation Acts forced Dissenters into becoming outsiders. Priestley, as always, took this belief of rational dissent to its most logical conclusion. He became a full-blown Socinian, later known as Unitarian, denying the divinity of Jesus Christ and viewing the worship of Christ as idolatrous. It was no wonder that he attracted so much opposition from churchmen.

For over a hundred years, religious tensions had been simmering between Anglicans and Dissenters, despite the 1689 Toleration Act. In fact, the term toleration was something of a misnomer. The preamble to the Act states that it was an act for "some ease to scrupulous consciences in the exercise of religion" [23]. The emphasis should be on the word *some*. The Act repealed neither the Act of Uniformity nor the Clarendon Code and merely exempted Dissenters from any of their penalties. During the passage of the Bill through the Commons, one Whig was heard to remark dryly that "the Committee, though they were for Indulgence, were for no Toleration" [24]. Furthermore, the aforementioned exemptions were only granted to Trinitarian Dissenters, explicitly excluding anti-Trinitarians (Socinians or Unitarians), Roman Catholics, Jews and even atheists.

Unitarians had even more cause for grievance after the 1698 Blasphemy Act was passed. This was specifically directed against any who denied the Trinity and a second offence could even result in three years imprisonment [25]. As a result of this, it could be argued that the Unitarians gradually replaced the Quakers as the Dissenting whipping boys of the established Church during the course of the Eighteenth Century.

Bishop Samuel Horsley, one of Priestley's main Anglican opponents. Birmingham City Archives, Priestley Collection by Samuel Timmins.

The Quakers had slowly lost their reputation for religious fervour over the course of the Eighteenth Century and had acquired a reputation for passiveness. They concentrated their attention on the removal of the burden of paying tithes by pressurising successive governments throughout the Century by the highly organised compilation of the Great Books of Sufferings [26]. For the Unitarians, however, any grievances were made even harder to bear when they were refused access to civil and military offices, and therefore any real political influence, under the Test and Corporation Acts. It was their agitation for the repeal of these acts, which would result in national and local tensions in Birmingham immediately prior to the 1791 Riots.

Although always mentioned together when discussing the dissenters' grievances, the Test and Corporation Acts were actually slightly different. Together, they presented formidable obstacles to Eighteenth Century Dissenters taking their places in society and ever fulfilling their full potential. The Corporation Act of 1661 required all holders of municipal offices to take the Oath of Allegiance and Supremacy, abjure the Solemn League and Covenant and, finally, to take communion in the Church of England. The last requirement effectively excluded all conscientious Dissenters from holding civil office. In practice, the effects of this could prove much worse as it was still possible for Dissenters to be elected to office by Anglican colleagues, whether in spite or not, and then to be fined for failing to serve [27]. The first Sampson Lloyd had had this very problem in 1696-7, when he was picked High Sheriff for the county of Herefordshire. He turned for help to his brother-in-law Ambrose Crowley junior, who was at the height of his wealth from his iron trade in London and had acquired some influence as a member of the Court of Common Council of the City of London. It was only through a lot of hard work that he was able to get Sampson discharged from the duty [28].

Less conscientious Dissenters could get round this thorny problem by occasionally conforming and attending Anglican Communion once a year. However, even this loophole was closed in 1711 when the Occasional Conformity Act was passed showing that resentment against Dissenters was still high. Furthermore, the Corporation Act was even further strengthened in 1673 when the Test Act was passed, requiring holders of all civil and military offices to sign a declaration against transubstantiation, in order to exclude Catholics from all government offices. A second Test Act was passed in 1678 as a result of anti-popery hysteria after the Titus Oates plot [29].

St Philip's Church, Birmingham, from the print by William Westley, 1732. Spencer Madan, the Rector of the Church, and Priestley engaged in a theological pamphlet war. Image from William Hutton, An History of Birmingham (1809 edition).

These two acts stood unrepealed for over a hundred years and were the causes of long standing grievances for both Dissenters and Catholics alike. Priestley believed in complete religious freedom for all and was naturally incensed by them. During the course of his increasingly acrimonious pamphlet dispute with Spencer Madan, Rector of St Philips Church in Birmingham, he set out his reasons for wanting their repeal and accused Madan of misleading the public into believing that the two Acts were necessary for the continuing survival of the Church of England. Priestley maintained that they were only necessary for the financial maintenance of corrupt churchmen [30]. Is it any wonder that Madan was incensed? Priestley later denied ever campaigning for the repeal of the Acts: "I was not particularly concerned in the conduct of it" [31]. It would seem that his memory could be extremely selective when it suited him.

Priestley was an extremely skilled writer, using considerable wit and humour to make his point. In the second of his *Familiar Letters*, he questions where Madan's principles had come from: "It must be from some very obscure quarter inaccessible to all mankind" [32]. Unfortunately, such was his wit that it only served to enrage further those who could not match him in sarcasm. The pamphlet war became more and more bitter and protracted on both sides, at times becoming very personal: "When men are treated like dogs, they will snarl at those who hold the whip over them, whether they receive a blow or not" [33].

There had already been considerable local tension over the struggle for control of the Birmingham Library, which had been very efficiently reorganised by Priestley since 1780. He had, before 1786, opposed the inclusion of any controversial books of any kind, whether written by himself or others. However, in 1786, a group of churchmen effectively took control of the running of the Library and forced a vote to include Priestley's *History of the Corruptions of Christianity*. Priestley immediately changed his stance to advocate the inclusion of all controversial writings. This change of heart was immediately manipulated against him to insinuate that he was just trying to force his own books into the Library. Priestley replied with his high-handed Address to the Subscribers of the Birmingham Library, which John Money has called " a prime example of his combative righteousness which his adversaries must have found so galling" [34].

Priestley first earned the nickname "Gunpowder Joe" in 1787, when an earlier work of his, *Reflections on the Present State of Free Inquiry in this Country*, was deliberately misquoted and taken out of context. The misquoted phrase, however, was ill advised in the extreme, especially as it was associated with the Gunpowder Plot on November 5th 1605. Priestley had been advised against including it by his great friend and editor, John Towill Rutt [35], but showed his usual stubbornness and independence of mind by insisting on its inclusion.

We are, as it were, laying gunpowder, grain by grain, under the old building of error and superstition, which a single spark may hereafter inflame, so as to produce an instantaneous explosion: in consequence of which, that edifice, the erection of which has been the work of ages, may be overturned in a moment, and so effectually that the same foundation can never be built upon again [36].

One could argue that the analogy could be employed against Priestley because of his numerous, deliberately inflammatory remarks. He seemed to delight in repeating the gunpowder analogy. In a letter to William Pitt, the young Prime Minister, he explained:

The gunpowder we are so assiduously laying grain by grain under the old building of error and superstition, in the highest regions of which they inhabit, is not composed of saltpeter, charcoal and sulphur, but consists of arguments; and if we lay mines with such materials as these, let them countermine in the same way [37].

Despite his protestations of peaceful intentions and methods, it was too late; the damage had already been done.

It could be argued that Priestley was merely headstrong or naïve and foolhardy. There is no doubt that his opponents seized upon his words and manipulated them but Priestley was not so gullible as some might think. F.W.Gibbs claimed that Priestley was continually prodded by some of his friends to go beyond his self-imposed limits of reason and argument [38], but it is highly unlikely that someone so independently-minded as Priestley would allow himself to be unduly influenced by others. Priestley was his own man, even if it lost him friends. Furthermore, it could be argued that Priestley was very well aware of the effect his words would have, especially on the masses. In 1790 in his *Familiar Letters Addressed to the Inhabitants of Birmingham, Letter III, On the Test and Corporation Acts,* Priestley claims that the church would procure a law to *banish* Dissenters, rather than *burn* them as had happened in previous centuries [39]. The emphasis is Priestley's. Was he in fact foreseeing the next year when his house would be burned and he would be banished from Birmingham, eventually even fleeing to America? It is hard to imagine that someone of his

The Repeal of the Test Act: A Vision, 1790.
From such implacable Tormentors
Fanatics, Hypocrits, Dissenters
Cruel in Power, and restless out
And when most factious,most devout
May God preserve the Church and Throne
And George the good that sits thereon
Nor may their Plots exclude his Heirs
From Reigning, when the right is theirs
For should the foot the head command
And Faction gain the upper hand
We may expect a ruin'd land Butler
Priestley Collection by Joseph Timmins,
Birmingham City Archives.

intelligence would not have had some idea of the animosity he would arouse with his ill chosen words. Later in the same letter he hinted that he might decide to flee the country if persecuted [40]. Again, was this suggestion prophetic? Throughout his *Familiar Letters* Priestley returns to the theme of gunpowder, unwilling to let the matter die a natural death: "Will the clergy seriously say that they are afraid of my arguments, and as much terrified at them, as they would be at real gunpowder? [41]

Priestley was undoubtedly deeply offended by some of the attacks upon his character. Indeed, it should be remembered that this was not a one sided fight, as Martin Smith has been careful to point out [42], but Priestley must shoulder his share of the blame for provocative writing. One of the worst examples of this was addressed to another of his opponents, Rev. Edward Burn: "I call upon you, sir, in the face of this town, and of your country, before whom you have published these accusations of me...To a charge of this serious nature, you must not sir be silent. I demand a distinct and explicit answer" [43].

Priestley had thrown down the gauntlet and effectively lit the gunpowder fuse. Did he get more than he expected in July 1791? Perhaps he got exactly what he expected. Was this why he showed so much calmness in the face of adversity?

Notes

1 Clark, John Ruskin, *Joseph Priestley: a comet in the system* (Torch Publications, USA, 1990).

2 Priestley, Joseph, *Familiar Letter addressed to the Inhabitants of Birmingham Letter XI Of Controversy* (Thompson, Birmingham, 1790) p 26.

3 Quoted *in Macmillan's Magazine 1874: Collected Essays III Joseph Priestley* (http://aleph0.clarku.edu/huxley/CE3/Priest.html), endnote 4.

4 Catherine Hutton's Letters, Birmingham Reference Library (afterwards BRL) 66997, p 24.

5 Quoted in Clark, op cit, p 19.

6 *Ibid,* p 20.

7 Quoted in Clark, op cit, p 15.

8 *Ibid,* p 24.

9 Smith, Martin, *Conflict and Society in late 18th Century Birmingham* Unpublished PhD thesis, University of Cambridge, 1977), deposited in Birmingham Reference Library) Appendix I pi.

10 Porter, Roy, *Enlightenment* (Allen Lane, Penguin, 2000) p 412.

11 *Ibid.*

12 Robinson, Eric, *New Light on the Priestley Riots* (*Historical Journal, Vol III, 1960*) p 73-75.

13 See Priestley, *Familiar Letters.*

14 Porter, *Enlightenment*, p 374-5, 413.

15 Smith, p 17. There is a full list of these tracts in his bibliography.
16 Coffey, John, *Persecution and Toleration in Protestant England 1558-1689* (Longman, 2000) p205; Porter, *Enlightenment,* p 412.
17 Porter, *Enlightenment,* p 409.
18 Quoted in i*bid.*
19 *Ibid.*
20 Jewitt ed., *The Life of William Hutton* quoted in Smith, p12.
21 Langford, Paul, *The Eighteenth Century* (Oxford University Press, Oxford) p 99.
22 Porter, Roy, *Flesh in the Age of Reason* (Allen Lane, 2003) p 363-4.
23 Coffey, op cit, p 199.
24 *Ibid.*
25 Coffey, op cit, p 200.
26 For details of religious tensions against the Quakers in Seventeenth-Century Birmingham, see Hill, Gay, *Religious Rivalries* (Unpublished MA thesis, University of Birmingham, 2003).
27 Coffey, op cit, p 168.
28 Lloyd, Humphrey, *The Quaker Lloyds in the Industrial Revolution* (Hutchinson, 1975) p 71-2.
29 Coffey, op cit, p 178.
30 See Priestley, *Familiar Letters III On Test and Corporation Acts.*
31 Quoted in Clark, op cit, p152.
32 Priestley, *Familiar Letters II,* p10.
33 Priestley, *Familiar Letters II On Test and Corporation Acts,* p 5.
34 Money, John, *Experience and Identity: Birmingham and the West Midlands 1760-1800* (Manchester University Press, Manchester, 1977) p 127.
35 Clark, op cit, p 154-5.
36 Quoted in *Ibid.*
37 Quoted in *Ibid.*
38 Gibbs, F.W., *Joseph Priestley: Adventurer in Science and Champion of Truth* (Thomas Nelson, 1965) p185.
39 Priestley, *Familiar Letters Letter III On Test and Corporation Acts,* p15.
40 *Ibid,* p 20.
41 Priestley, *Familiar Letters Letter VII Of Mr Madan's Letter to the Author,* p11.
42 See Smith, op cit, p 11-15 for a fuller description of this pamphlet war.
43 Priestley, Joseph, *Letters to the Rev. Edward Burn,* p 33-4, quoted in Smith, op cit, p15.

Chapter 5

JOSEPH PRIESTLEY:
TRAIL-BLAZING EXPERIMENTER

Goronwy Tudor Jones

The First Thirty-one Years

Joseph Priestley was born near Leeds in Yorkshire on 13th March 1733, and continued to live there until he became, at the age of 19, the first student to enrol at the new dissenting academy in Daventry. By the time he left about three years later, along with his main discipline, theology, he had studied philosophy, history, mathematics and science. Furthermore he had gained a working knowledge of six ancient and three modern languages. This formidable intellect was to become one of the most influential men of his time. His varied career took him to Needham Market in Suffolk (1755-58), Nantwich in Cheshire (1758-61), Warrington (1761-67), Leeds (1767-73) and Bowood House in Wiltshire (1773-80) before he came to Birmingham in 1780 for what he described as the happiest period of his life. This ended with the notorious Birmingham Riots of 14th July 1791, which forced Priestley and his family to flee to London. They remained there for two years before the continuing hostility

Print of Joseph Priestley, 1782, showing examples of scientific equipment beneath the portrait. Priestley Collection by Samuel Timmins, Birmingham City Archives.

31

towards his political and religious views led them, in August 1793, to emigrate to Northumberland, Pennsylvania. There, on 6th February 1804, Priestley died, never having returned to his native England. The same strong religious views were at the heart of Priestley's decision, at the age of 31 in 1765, to devote a considerable portion of his working life to science.

Before this, Priestley, an ordained minister, already had an international reputation for his contributions to the fields of language, history and education. In 1764, this was recognised when Edinburgh University awarded him a Doctor of Laws. He had by this time published the *Rudiments of English Grammar* (1761), which was in print for 50 years, and also *The Theory of Language, and Universal Grammar* (1762). His 1764 *Chart of Biography* – a very large sheet of paper, with the arrow of time running from left to right, upon which the famous names of history were meticulously placed in their appropriate places – was a huge success and was still in print in 1820. According to F W Gibbs:

...had he done no more than he had achieved by this time, he would have done enough to ensure a place in the annals of education ... Later, in his hands, the three main influences in education - the religious, the intellectual and the utilitarian – were combined to give what became the basic grammar school education over a long period.

The subjects he included as essential were Latin, English, French and mathematics, together with physics (natural philosophy) and chemistry. To the arts subjects he added history, to the sciences geography [1].

Our story begins in 1765 when we find the Reverend Joseph Priestley LL.D looking for a new challenge. He chose to embark on a history of science by beginning with a history of electricity. This was far more successful than Priestley had anticipated because he made important discoveries which launched him into the mainstream of the science of his day. Subsequent discoveries in what we now call biology, chemistry and respiratory physiology put him amongst the greatest scientific discoverers of history.

This paper, which analyses Priestley's science chronologically, begins with a brief discussion of his religious and metaphysical views, without which one cannot hope to do him justice. There follows a setting of the scientific scene in Priestley's time, emphasising the key ingredient, missing from Greek thought, that is at the heart of science as we now know it – experiment is the sole arbiter of scientific truth. We then follow Priestley from Warrington, where his pioneering work led to the first publication of the inverse square law of electrostatics, one of the few fundamental laws of physics, known today as Coulomb's law after the Frenchman who published it eighteen years later; to Leeds, where his work on gases, including the discovery that "plants purify air made noxious by animals breathing" led to his gaining the Copley Medal of the Royal Society; to Bowood House in Wiltshire, the home of the Earl of Shelburne, later Prime Minister, where he discovered oxygen and laid the foundations of the science of respiration; to Birmingham, where he performed the first recorded demonstration that water is not an element and continued his work on respiration.

Priestley's Religion and Metaphysics

First and foremost, Joseph Priestley was a minister of religion with views that were very unconventional in his day – he was a Unitarian, a Christian who rejected many of what he called the 'corruptions of Christianity' [2] taught by the Church of England. In the Unitarian tradition, he believed that theology should encompass the discovered truths of science, a position that is now quite acceptable to the Church of England. In view of the current interest in the relationship between religion and science, it is perhaps of interest to look in a little detail at one of the outstanding theological and scientific characters of his day. According to John Money [3], Priestley's beliefs were based on two tenets. Firstly, the existence of a benevolent God, whose works were not yet completed and who, therefore, manifested himself in a continuous act of infinite creation. Secondly, he denied absolutely that there was any difference between matter and spirit. Here Priestley is taking on board David Hartley's doctrine of the association of ideas. Hartley, influenced by the works of Newton, saw mental and emotional processes as having physical causes, just like the behaviour of inanimate planets. As pointed out by Jack Lindsay [4] in the introduction to Priestley's autobiography, in the 18th Century order in nature was considered as evidence for the existence of God. Money goes on to show that the first tenet implies to Priestley that God will be beneficent to mankind, which will eventually reach a state of unlimited happiness. For him, the pinnacle of this euphoric state is to act in conformity with the divine will. To arrive at this state, the Hartley doctrine (the second tenet) implies to Priestley that one must learn more and more about nature, not by theorizing, but by revealing nature through experimental discoveries. Eventually, a state will be reached when everyone, through this "pure revelation" of experiment, will know all things equally, what philosophers might term a state of absolute, utopian epistemological egalitarianism [5].

For Priestley then, the natural philosopher was something of a missionary explorer seeking the "hidden powers which the Deity had impressed upon matter." Again in his own words, "I view with rapture the glorious face of nature and I admire its wonderful constitution, the laws of which are daily unfolding themselves to our view." All this tells us that, to understand Priestley, it is essential to appreciate that, because of his religious belief about the divine nature of experimental revelation, he felt that he could best serve the community by moving rapidly from one discovery to another. As Gibbs points out[6]: "It was not his purpose to be side-tracked by any incidental observations, however intriguing. He was setting a trail. Others would pick it up, and in this way, natural knowledge would grow faster."

In fact, many clearly recorded important discoveries - in biology, chemistry, physics, and physiology – were left virtually untouched. Undoubtedly, one reason for this was the prejudice against his religious and political views – he was a liberal – that eventually led to the notorious 1791 Priestley Riots in Birmingham, during which his place of worship, his home, his laboratory and all his manuscripts were systematically destroyed. The absence of manuscripts may partly be responsible for the fact that Priestley's contributions are under-appreciated.

Setting the Scientific Scene

The natural philosopher or physicist of today has a very different picture of the universe from that of the Greeks. Aristotle taught that the universe was divided into two parts: the earthly region, a sphere with the earth motionless at its centre, extending almost to the moon; and the celestial region, again spherical, surrounding the earthly region. These regions were very different.

In the inner, earthly region, all things were made from four elements – earth, water, air and fire – and these were arranged in their proper places: earth, being the heaviest, at the core; next water, air and finally, uppermost, fire, being the lightest. Things are in a state of constant change and decay.

In the outer (celestial) region, there was but one, fifth element, sometimes called "quintessence" and sometimes "aether". All things being made of this, Aristotle argued that there could be no change or non-uniformity in the stars and planets. This region, also referred to as the "heavenly" sphere, is eternal and has divine qualities. It is composed of concentric divine spheres, beginning with the lunar sphere, the lowest and least divine, and working upwards through the solar sphere and the planetary spheres to the sphere of the fixed stars; outside this is the sphere of the Prime Mover or God.

This hierarchical natural philosophy of the Greeks, with everything having its designated place, was incorporated into the teachings of the Church, mainly by Saint Thomas Aquinas in the 13th Century, and is seen in the language of Shakespeare. In *King Lear*, Gloucester utters the words: "These late eclipses of the sun and moon portend no good to us". Adherence to the teachings of Aristotle hindered progress in science for about 2000 years. Even Galileo's discoveries establishing that there were mountains on the moon, that the sun had "blemishes" which we now call sun-spots, and the observation of Copernicus that the planets went round the sun, were not enough to eliminate Aristotle's influence. In 1624, a law was passed in France, which compelled the chemists of the Sorbonne to conform to the teaching of Aristotle on pain of death and confiscation of goods [7].

Nowadays, we do not divide the universe into two regions. We believe that matter out there in the cosmos and here on earth is made from the same constituents, governed by the same rules throughout. It was not always so: 400 years ago, in 1600, Giordano Bruno was burnt at the stake for arguing, on the grounds that the universe was created by one God, that physics here on earth and out in the cosmos should be the same.

So, atoms everywhere are made of negative electrons bound to positive nuclei by the Priestley/Coulomb electrical attraction, their detailed behaviour being governed by the rules of quantum mechanics and relativity. Nuclei are made up of neutrons and protons, which, in turn, are composed of even smaller particles called quarks. It is not known whether quarks are made of even more elementary building blocks. Discussions in modern biology without our knowledge of atomic behaviour would be unimaginable. Not only did Priestley first state the law that keeps the electrons near the atomic nucleus, he also had a hunch that electricity played an important part in chemistry.

Within the grand transition from the Greek view of matter to our current picture, there are several great sub-plots of science. In an attempt to put Priestley's discoveries into perspective we will mention three: firstly, the developments in astronomy made by people such as Copernicus, Kepler and Galileo were finally brought together by Newton in his *Principia*; secondly, there was the emergence of modern chemistry from alchemy in the latter half of the 18th Century; thirdly, in the same period, biology split into botany and zoology.

This emergence of modern science from Greek natural philosophy occurred around the time of the Reformation. The key ingredient that eluded the Greeks was experiment. Rationalism, based on logic and mathematics that the Greeks developed to a high level, is not enough. Science is based on the idea that any statement that disagrees with experiment is wrong. Experimental results, repeated and checked, are treated as objective truths. The cornerstone of science is experiment. No theory can ever be deemed absolutely true because not all experiments can ever be performed. When physicists talk of "laws of nature" such as Newton's "laws of motion", they no longer regard them as "universal laws", somehow obeyed by nature; how could a planet know Newton's "laws"? Rather, the scientists' "laws" are usually mathematical statements that summarise the results of experiments performed; particularly powerful "laws" also have a predictive power.

It is from the point of view of his contribution to making experimental discoveries about nature that we return to Joseph Priestley. "Let others *reason* better from the facts with which I supply them if they can: I shall listen to them with attention. But I cannot forbear observing, that I should be more obliged to them for the delivery of *more facts* from which to reason. *Speculation* is a cheap commodity. *New and important facts* are most wanted, and therefore of most value."

We will take things in chronological order, beginning with his work on electricity in Warrington.

Electricity in Warrington

After meeting Benjamin Franklin over the Christmas of 1765, and receiving great encouragement, Priestley set about his work with incredible energy. Based on his progress, he was elected to a Fellowship of the Royal Society in June 1766. By the end of the year, his 750-page book[8] *The History and Present State of Electricity, with Original Experiments*, was finished. In it, he records that on the 21st of December, "following the instructions of Dr Franklin" he verified that he could not take electricity from the inside of a charged metal cup, whereas he could from the outside.

Electricity. Electric Machines Plate VII from Abraham Rees, The Cyclopaedia or Universal Dictionary of Arts, Sciences, and Literature. Plates vol II. (London, Longman, Hurst, Rees, Orme and Brown, 1820). The illustration shows examples of machines for generating static electricity used by Priestley.

He then went on to interpret this by suggesting an inverse square law of electricity, by analogy with gravitation: "May we not infer from this experiment, that the attraction of electricity is subject to the same laws with that of gravitation, and is therefore according to the squares of the distances; since it is easily demonstrated, that were the earth in the form of a shell, a body in the inside of it would not be attracted to one side more than another" [9]. Since atoms consist of negative electrons held in the vicinity of positive nuclei by the inverse square law of electricity, a physicist must see this as a major contribution to science - even to the biological sciences since we are all made of atoms.

Earlier in the year, on 4th May 1766, Priestley recorded his discovery that charcoal conducts electricity. This was a significant discovery because, at the time, it was thought that only water and metals were conductors. From a biologist's point of view it is of interest to know why he was testing the electrical properties of charcoal. He had been using the charcoal to produce "mephitic air", a term used for unwholesome air in general and specifically for "fixed air" or carbon dioxide (CO_2). Priestley was trying to see if nature had a way of purifying "mephitic air", and had tried passing electricity through it – after all, we have lightning in the atmosphere. It did not, but Priestley, true to his quest to reveal the "secret powers which the Deity has impressed upon matter", did not miss the chance to study the electrical properties of charcoal.

We now move from Warrington to Leeds where Priestley embarked on the work on gases for which he is best known.

Leeds: Soft Drinks; Photosynthesis; Biology becomes Botany and Zoology

"It was a little after Midsummer in 1767, that I removed from Warrington to Leeds: and living, for the first year, in a house that was contiguous to a large common brewery, so good an opportunity produced in me an inclination to make some experiments on the fixed air that was constantly produced in it. Had it not been for this circumstance, I should, probably, never had attended to the subject of air at all."

Priestley's first major publications on gases created considerable excitement in the medical world. The unlikely source of this excitement was Priestley's discovery of how to "impregnate water with fixed air" (make fizzy drinks!) [10]. The reason for the excitement is explained in Priestley's pamphlet:

Sir John Pringle first observed, that putrefaction was checked by fermentation, and Dr. Macbride discovered that this effect was produced by the fixed air which is generated in the process, and upon that principle recommended the use of 'wort', as supplying a quantity of this fixed air, by fermentation in the stomach, in the same manner as it is done by fresh vegetables, for which he, therefore, thought that it would be a substitute; and experience has confirmed his conjecture.

At that time, Priestley's discovery of how to dissolve fixed air suggested that, "this great antiseptic principle may be administered in a variety of agreeable vehicles." Later, it was felt that fixed air might prevent scurvy, and Captain Cook took improved versions of Priestley's soda water making apparatus on his voyages. Fixed air does not cure scurvy but we can still remember Joseph Priestley as the father of the soft drinks industry.

We now come to the paper that gained Priestley the Copley Medal – the highest honour of The Royal Society. He had narrowly missed it for his work on electricity – because the relevance of the inverse square law was not yet fully appreciated. In the first paragraph of this paper entitled *Observations on Different Kinds of Air* [11], Priestley announces that "a considerable number of facts, which appear to me to be new and important, are sufficiently ascertained; and I am willing to hope, that when philosophers in general are apprised of them, some persons may be able to pursue them to more advantage than myself."

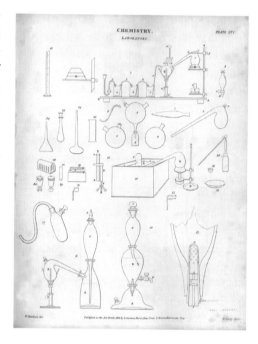

Chemistry Laboratory Plate XVI from Abraham Rees, The Cyclopaedia or Universal Dictionary of Arts, Sciences, and Literature. Plates vol. II (London, Longman, Hurst, Rees, Orme and Brown, 1820). The illustration shows examples of the chemical equipment that Priestley would have used for handling gases.

To put these discoveries in perspective it is helpful to have a picture of what was known at the time. It is remarkable that air was still, in 1772, generally regarded as a simple elementary substance – despite the fact that a considerable amount had been discovered about its properties. On the physics front, Galileo had shown that air had weight, Torricelli had measured the pressure of the atmosphere, and von Guericke had invented the pump. In chemistry, Boyle and others had shown that air had two components, one of which supported life. Various chemically different gases had been discovered. For example, Black had shown that "fixed air" (CO_2) was part of a solid – chalk – and could be obtained from it by the action of acids; the well-known test for fixed air was that it turned lime-water milky due to the chalk being restored. In addition, Cavendish had discovered "inflammable air" or hydrogen, as we now know it.

What was needed according to Brownrigg [12] was a systematic programme of research into the various "chemically different elastic fluids (gases) that were known; to consider those substances from which they are produced; by exact experiments to detect their properties when native and simple; to inquire what changes may result from their coalitions and combinations amongst one another..." This was the challenge that Priestley accepted: a voyage of discovery into the largely uncharted world of gases, almost all of which were invisible.

To begin with he made major improvements to the technology of handling gases and developed tests for recognising gases. This led to the discovery of new gases: "nitrous air" (nitric oxide or NO), "dephlogisticated nitrous air" (nitrous oxide, N_2O or laughing gas), "red nitrous vapour" (nitrogen dioxide or NO_2) and hydrochloric acid gas. Over the last decade, scientists have been surprised to find that nitric oxide has crucial physiological properties, the discovery of which led to the 1998 Nobel Prize in Medicine or Physiology. Although Priestley is mentioned in the Nobel Lectures as the discoverer of NO, there is no mention of his discovery that it had antiseptic properties.

Photograph of the statue of Joseph Priestley sculpted by Francis Williamson and unveiled in Birmingham in 1874. The statue symbolises Priestley conducting the scientific experiment which led to his discovery of "dephlogisticated air" or oxygen. Priestley focuses the rays of the sun through a lens which he directs towards a crucible which contains red oxide of mercury. He holds a test-tube above the crucible to collect the gas which is released during the experiment. Priestley Collection by Samuel Timmins, Birmingham City Archives.

While studying nitric oxide, Priestley observed that two volumes of nitric oxide and one volume of oxygen would yield two volumes of nitrogen dioxide. Here is an example of an important lead being left while Priestley continued his trail-blazing: a quarter of a century later we encounter "Gay-Lussac's Law of Combining Volumes" which states that when gases combine in a chemical reaction, the volumes involved are in the ratio of small numbers: Priestley had shown that two volumes of nitric oxide combine with one volume of oxygen to give two volumes of nitrogen dioxide. In the language of GCSE chemistry:

$$2NO + O_2 \rightarrow 2NO_2.$$

We now come to what is perhaps the major discovery of this classic paper: "Plants restore air that has been injured by respiration and burning." Let us enjoy Priestley's own description:

Accordingly, on the 17th of August 1771, I put a sprig of mint into a quantity of air, in which a candle had burned out, and found that, on the 27th of the same month, another candle burned perfectly well in it...

Several times I divided the quantity of air in which the candle had burned out, into two parts, and putting the plant into one of them, left the other in the same exposure, contained, also, in a glass vessel immersed in water, but without any plant; and never failed to find, that a candle would burn in the former, but not in the latter.

Later, on page 198:

These proofs of a partial restoration of air by plants in a state of vegetation, though in a confined and unnatural situation, cannot but render it highly probable, that the injury which is continually done to the atmosphere by the respiration of such a number of animals, and the putrefaction of such masses by both vegetable and animal matter, is, in part at least, repaired by the vegetable creation.

And, notwithstanding the prodigious mass of air that is corrupted daily by the above mentioned causes; yet, if we consider the immense profusion of vegetables upon the face of the earth, growing in places suited to their nature, and consequently at full liberty to exert all their powers, both inhaling and exhaling, it can hardly be thought, but that it may be a sufficient counterbalance to it, and that the remedy is adequate to the evil.

Priestley's old friend and mentor, Benjamin Franklin had seen this work in progress, and his enthusiastic letter to Priestley is included in the paper:

I hope this will give some check to the rage of destroying trees that grow near houses, which has accompanied our late improvements in gardening, from an opinion of their being unwholesome. I am certain, from long observation, that there is nothing unhealthy in the air of woods; for we Americans have everywhere our country habitations in the midst of woods, and no people on earth enjoy better health, or are more prolific.

So, when you next go to the garden to get a sprig of mint to boil with your potatoes, remember that it was with one of these that mankind realised that it will not suffocate in its own carbon dioxide!

This discovery also heralds a turning point in our understanding of the nature of life. Up until this time it was assumed that all living things made use of the air in a similar manner. This appreciation that plants use what we breathe out (CO_2) and we breathe in what they give out (O_2) captures the historic moment when biology split into botany and zoology. All this happened before Priestley and, independently, the Swede, Scheele, had isolated that constituent of air, which supports animal breathing and combustion – the gas we know as oxygen, but named "dephlogisticated air" by Priestley.

Bowood House, Wiltshire: Discovery of Oxygen; Respiratory Science

Priestley vividly describes how he heated what we now call mercuric oxide with his new 12-inch *burning lens* to discover *the most remarkable of all the kinds of air I have produced* [13]. He went on to say:

...this air is of exalted nature... A candle burned in this air with amazing strength of flame; and a red hot wood cracked and burned with a prodigious rapidity, exhibiting an appearance something like that of iron glowing with a white heat, and throwing sparks in all directions. But to complete the proof of the superior quality of this air, I introduced a mouse into it; and in such a quantity that, had it been common air, it would have died in a quarter of an hour; it lived, at two different times, a whole hour, and was taken out quite vigorous.

Priestley is best known for isolating the life-supporting element in the air, itself a truly romantic discovery. It was, however, more than that. The discovery of oxygen was a turning point in the quest to understand matter. Since the latter part of the 17th Century, the interpretation of experiments was influenced by the "phlogiston theory" of Becher and Stahl. It hardly deserves to be called a theory, but a last attempt to keep fire – the word phlogiston comes from the Greek word for fire - as an element.

Although he was aware of its limitations, Priestley continued to use the phlogiston idea, possibly because Lavoisier's formulation was also not the whole story, and said of the exalted gas (oxygen) that it "may not improperly be called dephlogisticated air". We shall see how Lavoisier improved Priestley's experiment to gain extra information, which enabled him to refute the phlogiston idea. This crucial experiment of Lavoisier's was one of two, both improvements on pioneering efforts by Priestley, which led to his foundation of modern chemistry [14]. The idea behind the phlogiston doctrine was that substances were made of phlogiston (the essence of fire) and ash. Good fuels such as candle-wax were rich in phlogiston and their burning was pictured thus:

$$\text{fuel} \xrightarrow{\textit{burning}} \text{ash + phlogiston} \quad (1)$$

Here we can see why Priestley called oxygen "dephlogisticated air" – it *attracts* phlogiston. The age-old process of getting metal from ore was pictured thus:

$$\text{ore + phlogiston (from fuel)} \xrightarrow{\textit{burning}} \text{metal} \quad (2)$$

It is ironic that the discovery of oxygen, which led to the overthrow of the phlogiston doctrine, was made by Priestley, one of the most eminent scientists to resist the demise of the old way of thinking. Cavendish was another.

What Lavoisier did first was to heat some tin with air in a sealed container (slow burning). He made two observations:

1   When he opened the container, air rushed in; he did not notice anything – phlogiston in particular – rushing out as (1) above would suggest.
2   The ash weighed more than the tin he started with – so phlogiston would need negative mass, which is impossible.

This marked the end of the phlogiston era, and with it the Aristotelian idea of fire as an element. The result of the experiment suggested to Lavoisier that when a substance burns in air it combines in some way with part or all of the air.

The next phase of his study sets out to determine something quantitative about the role played by air in the burning process. Lavoisier heated mercury in contact with a measured volume (V) of air and watched to see if the volume changed. He found that after the volume had gone down to 4/5 V, no further change took place. The remaining gas extinguished a lighted taper and suffocated animals put in it – he called the gas "azote", meaning "without life" in Greek; we now call it nitrogen. Lavoisier next took the residual ash (mercuric oxide) and heated it in the manner used by Priestley in his discovery of oxygen, and found that the volume of gas collected was 1/5 V – he had recovered what he had lost on heating the mercury. This gas vigorously supported life and burning - it was oxygen. So, at last, we have something that looks like modern science: when metal is heated or burnt, it combines with oxygen to form ash (oxide).

For those who like summaries:

> A man called Priestley from Brummagem
> Made his name by discovering oxygen.
> This paved the way
> For Lavoisier to say:
> Zut, on n'a pas besoin de phlogiston!

It was inevitable, that having isolated oxygen, Priestley would turn to the question of respiration. In 1776, and still at Bowood House, Priestley published a paper [15] entitled *Observations on Respiration and the Use of Blood*, which Gibbs refers to as the "beginnings of a scientific account of respiration". After a fascinating review of historical ideas on respiration, Priestley described experiments which show that "... respiration is a phlogistic ("chemical" in modern language) process affecting air in the very same manner as ... another phlogistic process... calcination ("oxidation") of metals...diminishing the quantity of it in a certain proportion, rendering it unfit for respiration or inflammation..." In this paper he shows that blood absorbs air, and even better, oxygen; this absorption takes place through serum and through animal membrane; blood goes red when it absorbs oxygen, and black if deprived of it. So, a large amount was established, much of it by Priestley, before Lavoisier began work on respiration (1777). Priestley was not even mentioned in several books on respiratory physiology, selected from the ones which were most used in the University of Birmingham's Medical School Library.

We now come to Priestley's spell in Birmingham, which he refers to as the happiest period of his life.

Birmingham: Water; more on Respiration

One of the reasons why Priestley was happy in Birmingham was that he had been invited to become a member of the Lunar Society of Birmingham, which became the leading scientific group in England in the decade between 1781 and 1791.

The story of the synthesis of water is one that has been surrounded by controversy because of its important role in the overthrow of the Greek view of the matter. This synthesis, together with the isolation of oxygen, were the crucial experiments that enabled Lavoisier to lay down the foundations of modern chemistry, ending the traditions of alchemy and phlogiston. [16] It would seem, therefore, appropriate to summarise the story of the water controversy by listing some key publications in chronological order.

In 1775, Priestley [17] reported on exploding a 1:2 mixture of oxygen and hydrogen: "with little more than one-third of highly dephlogisticated air, and the rest inflammable air, in the same phial, the report will be almost as loud as that of a small pistol; being, to judge by the ear, not less than forty or fifty times as loud as with common air." Anyone contemplating this experiment should take great care; ordinary test tubes will shatter! In 1781, Priestley [18] described repeating this "as a random experiment, made to entertain a few philosophical friends, who had formed themselves into a private society, of which they had done me the honour to make me a member." It was reported that, when the experiment was carried out in closed, clean, dry glass vessels, a dew was observed on the inside after the firing. The private society was the Lunar Society of Birmingham.

According to Schofield [19], "Cavendish caught the possible significance of some casual experiments made by Priestley and Warltire and instituted a series of experiments which might naturally lead him to a conclusion about the nature of water. These experiments were performed later in 1781 but were not published then."

On 26th April 1783, Watt interpreted an experiment by Priestley [20], which included the following: "Are we then not authorized to conclude that water is composed of dephlogisticated air and inflammable air, or phlogiston, deprived of their latent or elementary heat, and that dephlogisticated air or pure air is composed of water deprived of its phlogiston…?" [21]. Controversy exists about this letter, but the consensus seems to be that Watt was the first to postulate that water is a compound, without fully appreciating what it was a compound of.

Priestley's Airpump. The information on the brass plate notes "The airpump was made for Dr Priestley by Mr Harrison the employer of Sir Josiah Mason when a young man. Presented by Josiah Martyn Smith Esq". The pump was formerly in the possession of the University of Birmingham.

In June 1783, Priestley made public Cavendish's result – an accurate demonstration of the composition of water. Later in 1783, Lavoisier, who repeated Cavendish's experiment, came to the correct conclusion about the compound nature of water. Schofield concludes: "The experiments then were Cavendish's, the ultimate understanding was Lavoisier's ... Cannot Watt, at least, be granted his due: that he independently saw and reported the significant consequences of important experiments?" What about Priestley? There is no doubt that he was the first to synthesise water, no later than 1781. Priestley did not feel directly concerned in this controversy. He was more concerned with providing more experimental evidence. "In this business I am little more than the bellows blower."

Priestley, the trail-blazer, had already moved on. He was, by this time, getting involved with a new problem, arising from his activities using hydrogen: the iron from which it was being produced came in different forms - cast iron, steel, etc. – with different properties which he later showed were related to the amount of foreign matter in the iron; Priestley the metallurgist!

Cavendish and Lavoisier are usually credited with demonstrating that water is a compound, but the first recorded synthesis of water was in Birmingham. It may even have taken place in Soho House, the home of Matthew Boulton, which, in 1995, was renovated and opened to the public, looking as it did two centuries ago.

We finally come to a short paper [22] on respiration, which appeared in the Philosophical Transactions of the Royal Society in 1790, the year before Priestley was hounded out of Birmingham by an establishment-incited mob. Here Priestley recorded measuring the amount of oxygen breathed in and the amount of carbon dioxide breathed out: "I proceeded to ascertain how much fixed air (carbon dioxide) was actually formed by breathing a given quantity both of atmospherical and of dephlogisticated air (oxygen), in order to determine whether any part of it remained to enter the blood, after forming the fixed air." His discovery that the blood absorbed oxygen remained largely ignored for half a century because of Lavoisier's conjecture that respiration consists of combustion in the lungs, specifically the tubules, into which the blood secretes a humour (fluid) containing carbon and hydrogen, which yield carbon dioxide and water on combustion.

Conclusion

Some of Priestley's contributions to science have been presented, emphasising his outstanding contributions as an experimental scientist. His discoveries across the board, in biology, chemistry, physics, and physiology played a major part in those early days of science. They include: the first publication of one of the basic laws of physics, the Inverse Square Law of Electrostatics; the discovery that plants purify air made noxious by fire and animals breathing; the discovery of oxygen; the first recorded synthesis of water; pioneering experiments on the properties of blood.

A final word from Priestley:

The greater is the circle of light, the greater is the boundary of the darkness by which it is confined. But notwithstanding this, the more light we get, the more thankful we ought to be, for this means we have the greater range for satisfactory contemplation. In time, the bounds of light will be still farther extended: and from the infinity of the divine nature, and the divine works, we may promise ourselves. An endless progress in our investigation of them: a prospect truly sublime and glorious.

Notes
1 F. W. Gibbs, *Joseph Priestley* (Thomas Nelson and Sons, Ltd, London, 1965).
2 J. Priestley, *An History of the Corruptions of Christianity* (printed by Piercy and Jones for J Johnson, No. 72 St Paul's Churchyard, London, 1782).
3 J. Money, *Enlightenment and Dissent* 7 (1988) 69-89, and 8 (1989) 57-81.
4 J. Priestley, *Autobiography of Joseph Priestley*
   (Adams and Dart, Bath, England, 1970).
5 It is tempting to compare this with a statement from the epilogue in
   Stephen Hawking, *A Brief History of Time*
   (Bantam Press, London and New York, 1988).
   However, if we do discover a complete theory, it should in time be understandable by everyone, not just a few scientists. Then we shall all, philosophers, scientists, and just ordinary people, be able to take part in the discussion of the question of why it is that we and the universe exist. If we could find the answer to that, it would be the ultimate triumph of human reason – for then we would know the mind of God.
6 Gibbs, *op.cit.*
7 L. Hogben, *Science for the Citizen*
   (George Allen and Unwin Ltd., London, 1959), p. 402.
8 J. Priestley, *The History and Present State of Electricity*
   (J Doddsley, J Johnson, B Davenport, and T Cadell, London, 1767).
9 For a detailed discussion see G. Tudor Jones, "In Praise of Joseph Priestley – the Particle Physicist!", *Physics Education* 26, 1991, pp.147-152.
10 J. Priestley, *Directions for Impregnating Water with Fixed Air:*
   In order to communicate to it the peculiar Spirit and Virtues of Pyrmont Water, and other Mineral Waters of a Similar Nature
   (London, 1772. Dedication dated Leeds, 4th of June 1772).
11 J. Priestley, "Observations on different Kinds of Air",
   Philosophical Transactions of the Royal Society , 62, 1772, pp.147-264.
12 Gibbs, *op.cit.*

13 Priestley, "Observations on different Kinds of Air", op.cit.

14 A-L. Lavoisier, *Traite elementaire de chimie* (Paris, 1789).

15 J Priestley, in *The Philosophical Transactions of the Royal Society*, 1776, pp.226-248.

16 J. R, Partington, *A History of Chemistry*, Volume 3 (Macmillan and Co Ltd, London, 1962); R. E. Schofield, "Still more on the water controversy", *Chymia* 9, 1964, pp.71-76.

17 J. Priestley, Experiments on Different Kinds of Air, Volume 2, (J. Johnson, No. 72 St. Paul's Church-yard, 1775), p. 99.

18 J. Priestley, Experiments and observations relating to various branches of natural philosophy, Vol 2, (Printed by Pearson and Rollason, for J Johnson, No. 72, St. Paul's Church-yard, London, 1781) pp. 395-398.

19 Schofield, *op. cit.*

20 *ibid.*

21 Letter, James Watt to Joseph Priestley, 26th April 1783, Birmingham City Archives.

22 J Priestley, *The Philosophical Transactions of the Royal Society*, 1790.

Chapter 6

JOSEPH PRIESTLEY AND HIS INFLUENCE ON EDUCATION IN BIRMINGHAM

Dr Ruth Watts

Joseph Priestley, celebrated as a great creative scientist but infamous in his day for his radical stance in both theology and politics, was also a progressive educationalist who influenced educational developments both nationally and in Birmingham where he lived from 1780 to 1791. Priestley promoted an environmentalist and rational philosophy of education, underpinned by his experience firstly as a schoolteacher, then as an innovative lecturer in an astonishing range of subjects at the liberal dissenting academy of Warrington, and from 1791 to 1794 a lecturer in science and history at Hackney Academy in London [1]. This article will examine Priestley's educational philosophy briefly and then see how far it was typical of Priestley's fellow "Lunaticks" and how adherents to Priestley's ideas translated them into action in Birmingham.

Priestley's Educational Philosophy

People, Priestley insisted, were not what they were born but what their education had made them. A careful education from birth in all aspects of being - intellectual, moral and physical - was a prerequisite, therefore, for the virtuous, useful and happy man or woman. Priestley derived his ideas partly from John Locke who was admired by many dissenting educationalists and, indeed, others, but even more so from David Hartley whose *Observations on Man* he reissued in condensed form. He admired the clarity and coherence of Hartley's associationist psychology, which maintained that all complex or 'intellectual' ideas arise from simple ones, which, in turn, were formed from external impressions made on the senses [2]. Priestley eagerly proclaimed thus people developed through individual associations and circumstances [3] - "children may be formed or moulded as we please" [4]. Reflection, experience and extensive intellectual education were what was needed for people to attain moral, religious and intellectual progress and even perfection not innate cause or divine intervention [5].

Thus it appeared that people of both sexes should receive the same, careful, wide education and that parents and teachers in particular should fully understand associationist psychology and be well-educated themselves. This education should be scientific in method and in content. Thus empirical and experimental subjects such as modern history and science were extolled, both new subjects in higher education and in schools [6]. Priestley's own teaching and writings also helped the acceptance of English and its literature as an academic subject in both schools and academies [7]. With sublime optimism in the beneficial effects of the curriculum and methods he disseminated, Priestley urged teachers to illustrate and exemplify their ideas and introduce systematic methods [8]. He anticipated the use of sources in history teaching and of experiment in science teaching way ahead of his time, adding that all studies should be adapted to the age and the capacity of the learner [9].

JOSEPH PRIESTLEY, LL.D.;F.R.S.

Print of Joseph Priestley with images of children. Priestley Collection by Samuel Timmins, Birmingham City Archives.

Priestley, indeed, applied his science of psychology throughout learning. He saw particular kinds of knowledge as power - power to create virtuous beings and to control the forces of nature for good. To him science was that paradigm of free enquiry, which was of "peculiar concern" to his religious group, the Unitarians, and fitted his perception of the needs of the rising industrial and commercial middle-class in which many dissenters, including the energetic Unitarians, were to be found [10]. Excited that it was an era of dramatic change for humanity, of "new light ... bursting out in favour of the civil rights of men", Priestley was also well aware of the concerns of those who were leading the industrial revolution. With Matthew Boulton, James Watt, Josiah Wedgwood (another Unitarian) and others, Priestley was an active participant in the scientific, industrial and educational concerns of the small but vital Lunar Society of Birmingham. Priestley was certain that the leaders of the future would come from those who had mastered the sources of knowledge which had changed the world [11]: thus, to him, the very scientific and industrial interests, which were scorned in the traditional education of Oxbridge and the public schools, were the just basis of a prosperous meritocracy [12]. For him, literary *and* scientific excellence including modern languages accompanied by a proper moral development were necessary in a "truly liberal education" which would produce enlightened leaders of the middle-class [13]. Thus through his teaching and prolific writings he urged a new liberal and useful education, throughout his life.

Priestley was a dramatic and innovative force in education. In Birmingham he had particular effect firstly on the Unitarians through his preaching at the New Meeting and teaching in the Sunday school; secondly through his part in the setting up of the library; and, thirdly on all his family and friends particularly those in the Lunar Society including the children of members who visited his house and ran freely through his laboratory and library [14].

Richard Lovell Edgeworth, member of the Lunar Society, inventor and writer. The educational publication, Practical Education was written with his daughter, Maria. Local Studies and History, Birmingham Central Library.

The Lunar Society and Education

Priestley is perhaps known best in Birmingham today through his involvement with the Lunar Society, in which, from 1780 to 1791, he was a leading light. This small but dynamic group of creative scientists, enterprising inventors and business men and innovative writers are best remembered for their scientific and technological advances. In the history of education, however, the educational significance of Lunar Society figures such as Joseph Priestley, Richard Edgeworth, Thomas Day and Erasmus Darwin, (and I would add Maria Edgeworth since she wrote with her father), within late Eighteenth Century radical and progressive education has been trumpeted since the 1960s [15]. The Lunar Society itself was an educative society, in the way that its members eagerly exchanged ideas, excitedly caught up and developed each other's suggestions and enthusiastically engaged in a range of subjects upon which they poured their increasing expertise. When Matthew Boulton proudly said, "I sell, Sir what all the world desires to have – POWER" [16], he was referring to Soho's manufacture of Watt's steam engines, which revolutionised industry in more than one sense of the word. He could as easily have been referring to knowledge for he and his friends were rapidly increasing human knowledge and they were keenly aware of the power that that could give them. Priestley urged, "In fact it is *knowledge* that finally governs mankind, and *power* ... must at length yield to it" [17]. Thus to possess the type of knowledge which could command power in the world became a key objective of reformers in the late eighteenth and nineteenth centuries. Education was therefore one of the subjects some of them studied so keenly.

Lunar Society member, Thomas Day, humanitarian poet and writer, who tried to introduce Rousseau's educational ideas into English society. His book, Sandford and Merton, remained a popular children's book into the Nineteenth Century. Local Studies and History, Birmingham Central Library.

Dissatisfied with the limited, traditional classical education which was common fare for boys of the upper and middle classes and which looked backwards to the triumphs of past civilizations, rather than forward to the achievements of the new, members of the Lunar Society believed in a new modern and scientific education. They showed their advanced ideas through the education they gave to their own children at home or through the most progressive institutions they could find in Britain or on the continent [18]. The chief educationalists in the Society published educational works to diffuse their ideas. Two of them had practical experience of teaching, Priestley, as seen above, and Richard Edgeworth, who educated his nineteen children by his four successive wives at home. All the Lunatick educationalists agreed on a rational education, which enabled children and students to think for themselves, to back their ideas with evidence and to replace rote learning with a practical understanding of how things were or worked. The knowledge they so deeply desired was scientific both with regard to content and method. They wanted to understand in every way the world in which humans lived. They might retain classics for a "gentleman's education", but devote far less time on them, preferring instead to study 'modern' subjects including not only science and its application, but modern history based on sources, English literature and modern languages. They were not against the arts but fused them with science to produce a new culture. This was exemplified in Wedgwood's pottery and Darwin's poetry [19].

In opposition to traditional educationalists, Lunaticks positively rejoiced in science and technology, wanting to harness nature for the use of humanity. They were humane in intent, for example, they were anti-slavery despite the fact that the profits of Birmingham business, which was so important to Boulton especially, were bound up with the slave-trade. The coins and medals struck at Soho by Boulton and Wedgwood's cameos [20] for the anti-slave trade campaign demonstrated the liberal, reforming impulse so richly exemplified by Priestley.

The revolutionary nature of this must be emphasised. Science, however interesting as entertainment, was usually dismissed in traditional education as merely a hobby for amateurs, a study for classes below the rank of 'gentlemen'. But the Lunaticks and their friends were those who were turning Britain into the first modern industrial nation and were positive that the leaders of the future would come from those who had mastered the sources of knowledge which had changed the world. This, together with literary excellence and moral development formed a "truly liberal education" [21] and, in turn, would forge a

Dr Erasmus Darwin, doctor, scientist and poet and friend of Priestley's in the Lunar Society. His Plan for the Conduct of Female Education in Boarding Schools reflected contemporary interest in the education of middle-class girls. Local Studies and History, Birmingham Central Library.

new type of gentleman - enterprising, open to new ideas, tolerant, humane, liberal and civic-minded in contrast to what they saw as privileged, duelling, pleasure-loving, selfish aristocrats. This was a middle-class emphasis but the type of education could hopefully be translated to all.

The concept was essentially male, but the Lunaticks extended such ideals to women too - perhaps as revolutionary a thought as any others they had. Richard Edgeworth's second wife, Honora Sneyd, for example, was the inspiration for some of his educational methods. His eldest daughter Maria worked with him and became a famous author and educationalist in her own right. Both Richard and Maria wanted women to develop fully their powers of reasoning and judgement and thus included many illustrations of girls engaged in experiments and reasoning in their trilogy, *Practical Education* [22]. Erasmus Darwin, although more sentimental, agreed with such aims in his book on female education written for his own two illegitimate daughters who were establishing a school in spacious surroundings in Ashbourne in 1792. His attention to a healthy, stimulating educational diet for girls extended to taking older ones to see the modern wonders of the English world - the cotton, pottery, iron and other industries of the midlands and the north [23]. Another Lunar member, the Quaker manufacturer and chemist, Samuel Galton junior, with his wife educated their daughter Mary in science, classics, languages, literature, history and modern politics, wood-carving, book-binding and model and chart making. Her later turn to evangelical religion led her to criticise this early education for its licence, its gender egalitarianism and its corrupting influences, particularly the over-reliance on human reason of her former friends the Unitarian Priestleys [24]. Such a view was more typical of most in the early Nineteenth Century than those of the Lunar Society. The rational, useful, scientific, liberal, (middle-class) education they desired was revolutionary for its time and was hugely contested at a time of revolutionary and then national wars with France. This can be seen in the Birmingham experience in the Nineteenth Century.

Maria Edgeworth, the daughter of Priestley's friend R. L. Edgeworth and an important writer on educational subjects. Local Studies and History, Birmingham Central Library.

Birmingham: Priestley's Educational Inheritance

It was from the Unitarians (rational dissenters who rejected both the trinity and original sin), who met in Priestley's chapel, the New Meeting and its sister the Old Meeting, that many of those in Birmingham influenced by his teaching, came.

A member of the Brotherly Society, a joint society of the teachers from the boys' Sunday schools of the two Meetings, was William Matthews who had become a Unitarian after hearing Priestley speak at the Society and, to his own astonishment, finding him to be "placid, modest and courteous, pouring out, with the simplicity of a child, the great stores of his most capacious mind to a considerable number of young persons of both sexes, whom ... he encouraged to ask him questions ... if he advanced anything which wanted explanation, or struck them in a light different from his own" [25]. The largely working class Brotherly

Society, established in 1796 to train teachers from among the boy pupils, ran schools which attracted many pupils because of their emphasis on a broad secular education - an emphasis as unusual at the time as its democratic organisation. This society itself had grown out of an older one, established whilst Priestley was still minister, which gave both a more extensive education to youths who had left the Sunday school and lectures on science and mechanics to factory workers. The members also ran a debating society and constructed scientific apparatus themselves to investigate the principles of mechanics, hydrostatics, electricity, gases and astronomy. In 1794 and 1795, a member, David Jones, who later became a barrister, delivered "some admirable courses of lectures" on Hartley's theory of the mind, attended by large numbers of both sexes from different denominations.

Lunar Society member, Samuel Galton junior, who educated his daughter, Mary, according to Priestley's ideas. Local Studies and History, Birmingham Central Library.

A member of this Society, Thomas Clark, gave scientific lectures in his own home to artisans (the more skilled manual workers), several of whom worked at the Eagle foundry and so they were nicknamed the "cast-iron philosophers". One of these, Josiah Pemberton was an early gas-light inventor. Clark himself had made his own fortune through a simple invention of winding balls of cotton he made to further his wife's fancy goods business. An attender at Priestley's Sunday classes, he later ran a school himself. Another philanthropist who gave free lectures in his own house to artisans was the Unitarian Thomas Carpenter. He and his brother Samuel founded the valuable Artisans Library to which artisans could belong for a small subscription, although this would be sufficiently large for a workman's wage to ensure that only the better-off were likely to join. The participants recalled such ventures with great pride. Apparently, they were all for men and undoubtedly the most spectacular Unitarian educational initiatives were. Women, however, were allowed into meetings as Matthews' tribute to Priestley quoted above indicates [26].

Middle-class benefactors included Thomas Ryland whose family intermarried with Clark's. The religious, social and political interests of each family were intermingled from Priestley's time onwards [27]. Other ventures such as the "Philosophical Institution" founded in 1800-1, where men like Thomas Wright Hill lectured on science, led Matthews in 1827 to laud the enlightened spirit of Birmingham men of business and the resulting orderly population: "Birmingham may probably be adduced as one of the most striking instances and strongest proofs of the civilizing and moral effects of education, that characterize modern times" [28].

Such ventures, then and now, have been criticised for their paternalistic attitudes and certainly there was a gulf between the seemingly egalitarian activities of the Brotherly Society and the increasingly wealthy and professional members of the Old and New Meetings such as the Kenricks, Rylands and Oslers. The Brotherly Society itself is most remembered for helping to educate men like Thomas Wright Hill who became its president and James Luckcock, later prominent in progressive Unitarian Sunday school

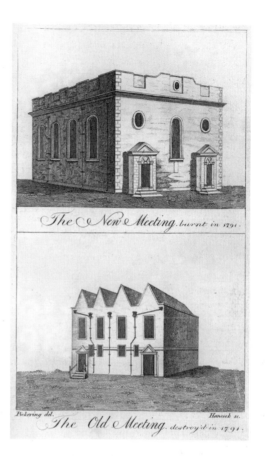

The Old and New Meeting Houses, the Unitarian chapels in Birmingham. William Hutton, An History of Birmingham (Birmingham, 1809). Local Studies and History, Birmingham Central Library.

education and a prosperous manufacturer. On the other hand, what must be remembered is that those middle-class businessmen themselves who engaged in these educational ventures were struggling both against the prejudices of the landed upper and middle classes who regarded them not as gentlemen but uneducated philistines and against those of their own kind who saw education beyond fourteen as incompatible with a "sufficient application to business". In contrast men like Thomas Wright Hill, who lectured on science and mathematics, argued that further education was far more useful than the pursuits with which young men in business usually occupied themselves [29].

From Priestley to the Hills

Thomas Wright Hill was a true heir of Priestley, being converted to Unitarianism from strict Calvinism when young and becoming a member of Priestley's congregation in Birmingham. Ardent, inventive, guileless and unconventional, his friends said of him that he had every sense except common sense. Both he and his future wife, Sarah Lea, showed courage in defence of Priestley following the 1791 Birmingham Riots. Thomas was fascinated by science to the point of eccentricity. It was his wife's sagacity that kept the family afloat and it was her persuasion that led to Thomas taking over Thomas Clark's school and opening Hill-Top, a secondary school for boys, in 1803 because she wanted her growing family to receive a better education than they could afford otherwise [30].

The Hill children of five brothers and two sisters received constant, eager discussion and debate at home, through self-education and through the hard discipline of teaching. From the age of thirteen each of the sons became a pupil-teacher at Hill-Top. Edwin, Rowland and Arthur successively worked part-time in the Birmingham Assay Office as well, gaining first-hand experience of metal-working and engineering, whilst engaging in developments in education. Many in the fierce educational debates of today might welcome this mixture of practical, vocational and intellectual education. The Hill youths, indeed, appeared to have turned from scientific experiment to practical engineering to intellectual discovery with an alacrity and intensity reminiscent of the old Lunar Society but almost frightening in ones so young. Determined on self and mutual improvement, it was Matthew and Rowland who rectified their lovable father's want of method and it was Rowland who chiefly laid the principles of their new school of 1819, Hazelwood [31].

Hazelwood was to become a brilliant showplace of almost revolutionary ideas in education for the time. The Hill family always acknowledged their debts to others, however, and of these the principal were Priestley and Maria Edgeworth. Harry Armytage termed the amazing school system of the Hill family as an "educational refraction of Priestley's ideas" [32]. The "Great Maria" had become one of the most well-known novelists of the day especially for her tales for children in which she combined moral and practical education in fictional form. The Hills admired her deeply. Matthew attributed his egalitarian views on women partly to reading her *Modern Griselda* and he and Rowland gratefully acknowledged their debt to her ideas and principles on education in their own treatise of 1822, which became known as *Public Education*. Rowland visited her in Ireland and remembered with pride how in his youthful poverty he saved up to buy her *Parent's Assistant*, a purchase later emulated by his brother Frederic and sister Caroline [33].

Maria Edgeworth and the Hills developed those principles of education so eagerly debated in the Lunar Society. The Hazelwood experiment was unique, however. Run by the astonishingly talented Hill family, its aim was useful, pupil-centred education which would give its scholars sufficient knowledge, skills and understanding to allow them to continue self-education through a life "most useful to society and most happy to himself" [34].

A "Modern" Education

Unlike the Edgeworths, the Hills believed that older children, especially boys, could be taught better and more efficiently in large schools. They extolled the skills of good teaching which stimulated "clear, vivid and accurate conceptions" through the association of ideas through drama, costume, models, maps, illustrations, diagrams etc. and gave learners the encouragement of repeated success [35].

These principles, so reminiscent of Priestley and the Edgeworths [36], were illustrated in numerous ways. The pupils were setted for subjects according to ability and taught as much as possible through the senses. Drama was used extensively throughout the curriculum. Modern languages were learnt orally first; mathematics and science were learnt through practical experiments and mental arithmetic practised to a fantastic level. An example of the boys' practical ingenuity was given in 1819 when they made a complete survey of Birmingham, making extensive use of trigonometry, arithmetic and mensuration whilst doing so and devising practical methods to sustain accuracy. They even invented a new mode of using a theodolite in doing this. This was certainly applied knowledge and understanding on a "Lunatick" scale [37].

Print of Hazelwood School. Local Studies and History, Birmingham Central Library.

The sheer delight, which the Hill brothers had in science and technology, was also demonstrated in the curriculum although these subjects did not dominate it. The Hills were neither so narrow nor so unaware of the likely wishes of their patrons to have that. But they did give status, thought and an eager welcome to these subjects only seen in that period in a few schools run by like-minded teachers. Their commitment was shown in 1829 when they appointed Edward Brayley, a reputed science lecturer, whose excitement, joy and enthusiasm in the new inventions and science of the day was evident. In 1831 his *The Utility of the Knowledge of Nature considered: ...* described his teaching at the Hills' schools in detail. Experiments were plentiful in the purpose-built laboratory at Hazelwood, which, like the gymnasium, was an unusual provision at that time [38] [39].

Furthermore, the whole system was designed to produce order, self-discipline, initiative and self-activity, those qualities vital to an energetic, entrepreneurial, successful commercial middle-class. Corporal punishment was considered demeaning to self-respect and gradually dropped altogether. Instead, an elaborate banking system based on receiving or giving counters or marks as a reward or punishment taught boys the value of work, effort and money all together [40]. The teaching and, indeed, the entire system, encouraged a large amount of pupil participation.

Such principles made Hazelwood a regular showplace for distinguished visitors who longed for the reform of middle-class schooling [41], yet the middle-class generally was largely unappreciative of the schoolboy republic and suspected the owners' political liberalism and undogmatic religion. Although Arthur Hill headed Bruce Castle, a less radical offshoot of Hazelwood in London, from 1833 for thirty-four years, Hazelwood closed in 1833 and therefore could hardly become the basis of a national system, as its founder had so deeply desired. Even some ex-students thought the boys were pushed into being "premature men" who priggishly assumed they "could amend everything from education to driving a horse" [42]. Nor did their hard won talents automatically earn them the status of an educated gentleman amongst the more traditionally educated as even Rowland Hill found to his acute disappointment [43].

Nevertheless, the school was responsible for educating many of Birmingham's Nineteenth Century elite, "gentlemen" in Birmingham at least. The Hills themselves, united in all they did, were extraordinarily prolific in invention and reform of all kinds including Rowland, inventor of the penny postage stamp, and Edwin, inventor of amazing machines at both the Post Office and at home. Matthew Davenport Hill became a barrister and Recorder of Birmingham. Local pupils included an impressive array of inventors, scientists, liberal politicians and local leaders including a number of the twenty-three Unitarian mayors of Birmingham between 1841 and 1893. Just one example was Follet Osler who constructed a model of the Hazelwood heating system whilst still at the school where he also helped print the *Hazelwood Magazine*. His glassworks in Icknield Street was

Mrs Joseph Priestley, by C. F. von Breda, oil on canvas.
Soho House, Birmingham Museums and Art Gallery.

A PRIEST OF LIBERTY.

"Every Man has his Price."—Sir R. Walpole.

THE present subject of our pictorial stricture, is professedly, and in the fullest sense of the word, a Revolutionist; a kind of epicure in politics, rather studious to vary the cookery of dishes, so as they may suit his whimsically depraved appetite, than to provide a wholesome meal of any: with whom liberty is considered as a licence not granted, but taken. A leveller, who feeling no workings in his own breast, which would raise him to a situation of trust in a government, exiling in meritorious subordination, is for throwing down all distinctions; that honours no longer attaching themselves to virtues, all alike may have an equal chance for power; the intermediate links in society between the most lawless subject and the most lawful sovereign being broken, all who have no law of conscience, may, in their turns, become tyrants, and kings become slaves.

He is a sworn enemy to all tests, as they call for a confession of faith, which is supposed to influence practice, and direct an obedience to ruling powers.

His religion is wedded to his politics, and his philosophical morality is the amiable offspring. Without faith in the sacred text, which he profanes by quotation, he can exclaim, with the fervour of an apostle, "Lord, now lettest thou thy servant depart in peace!" in the midst of anarchy and bloodshed!

As a philosopher, he surveys mankind in masses, and only listens to the inarticulate shouts of the multitude; the individual complaint of suffering virtue are lost in the clamour; and private calamity he considers as public good.

Such is the man, and such are the principles that attach him to the cause of humanity. The value of such abilities to the public, it would be yet more difficult to ascertain; for though they have been many years offered to sale, and puffed off with all the legerdemain of literary cabal, they have not yet been seriously bid for by any party.

c.

The Attic Miscellany. 1790.

THE PHLOGISTICATED DIVINE.

See the Embellishment.

HAVING already presented the Public with a just character of this religious and political Insect, we should not trouble ourselves or them with a second edition, but that the phlogistic spirit of the times, and a late accident, recals him to our recollection. Upon the news arriving of the French king's capture, the Doctor was seized with emotions of joy so strong and convulsive, as to make his friends apprehend some dangerous consequences. Whether they supposed that his gentle spirit would soar to the ethereal frontiers of pure peace and bliss, there to meet the immaculate troops which his divine and orthodox precepts have detached before him—whether it would hover over the patriotic bands of Paris, which his political doctrines have inspired—or whether upon a beam of his own elastic fire it would be sent express to the more congenial phlegmonious abyss to which that arch Dissenter, LUCIFER has been so many centuries consigned before him—was not for their narrow comprehensions—it was sufficient for them to say and hope that, as his merits were singular, so would his rewards be distinguished; and, that for great a man, however corporally removed from this immensity of human action, should die in the recollection of free born Briton, they composed the following

EPITAPH.

Here lies a Priest of priestley name,
Whose claims, alas! on earthly fame
    Dull destiny deny'd—
Since, had his worth been duly prais'd
On high his corpse had now been rais'd,
    And not to worms allied.

Should any doubt his patriot zeal
To freedom and the public weal,
    To Stanhope such may turn;
Stanhope, with equal glowing breast,
Departed virtue shall attest,
    And consecrate his urn.

*Left. Political Portraiture No. 3 Political Gunpowder. Priestley Collection
by Samuel Timmins, Birmingham City Archives.
Right. Political Portraiture No. 4 Dr Phologiston. Priestley Collection
by Samuel Timmins, Birmingham City Archives.*

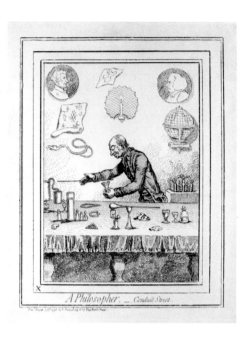

A Philosopher. Priestley Collection by Samuel Timmins, Birmingham City Archives.

Magnetic Dispensary. Priestley Collection by Samuel Timmins, Birmingham City Archives.

The Death and Pain and P.......y. A reference to Priestley's fellow radical Tom Paine.
Priestley Collection by Samuel Timmins, Birmingham City Archives.

The Treacherous Rebel and Birmingham Rioter.
Priestley Collection by Samuel Timmins, Birmingham City Archives.

Mr Burke's pair of Spectacles for short sighted politicians. Edmund Burke was a conservative writer who attacked the writings and actions of radicals in print.
Priestley Collection by Samuel Timmins, Birmingham City Archives.

The Friends of the People. Priestley Collection by Samuel Timmins,
Birmingham City Archives.

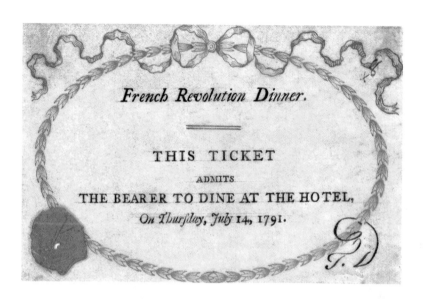

French Revolution Dinner. This Ticket admits the bearer to dine at the Hotel on Thursday, July 14th, 1791. No. 48. Initialled T.D. French Revolution Dinner. Priestley Collection by Samuel Timmins, Birmingham City Archives.

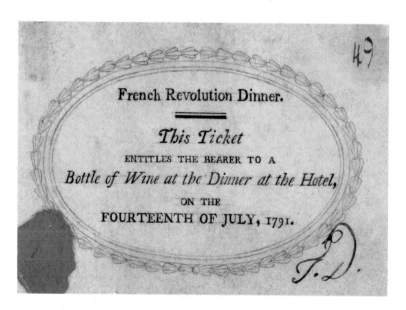

French Revolution Dinner. This Ticket entitles the bearer to a Bottle of Wine at the Dinner at the Hotel on the Fourteenth of July, 1791. No. 49. Initialled T.D. Priestley Collection by Samuel Timmins, Birmingham City Archives.

Middletown, Connecticut, in a watercolour painted by Miss M. Russell, c.1800. If the date is correct it must have been done by Mary, because Martha married in 1798 and returned to England in 1799. It is the earliest known drawing of any Connecticut town. Reproduced by kind permission of The Connecticut Historical Society, Hartford, Connecticut.

Joseph Priestley House, Northumberland, Pennsylvania, U.S.A. Photograph by courtesy of the Joseph Priestley House Pennsylvania Historical Museum Commission.

celebrated nationally for pioneering sheets of glass up to 20 feet high. His Crystal Fountain at the Great Exhibition of 1851 was considered to be one of the scientific achievements of the day. He invented many useful machines and ingenious clocks including the town clock, "Big Brum". His secret donations included £10,000 to the fledgling University of Birmingham [44].

Liberalism

A further illustration of their Priestleyan inheritance was given in the way the Hills and their ex-pupils were engaged in a whole plethora of social and political reform including the 1832 Reform Act, the Anti-Corn Law League and anti-slavery agitation. The Hill brothers themselves were prominent in Post Office and prison reform. It was not surprising they were reformers. Their older relatives had been supporters of the French Revolution along with Priestley in the 1790s and some had suffered with him. Their education, after all, was in citizenship. They all knew each other and were intermarried. Many were Unitarians [45].

An Educative Society

Such inter-connections helped these families to fight for educational and other reforms together, although it proved difficult to establish either dissenting rights in public education or a liberal, modern scheme of education for the commercial middle-classes [46]. Greater success was achieved in adult education in Birmingham although this did take time. Difficulties of financing institutions dependent on middle-class private patronage and the fees of low paid workers were exacerbated in Birmingham, as elsewhere, by the patronising attitudes and selfish economic dictates of supposedly liberal and radical educational benefactors who alienated the very people they most wanted to attend. Even otherwise humanitarian reformers such as Matthew Davenport Hill could be guilty of this, but he did support technical education, only as long as the working-class was not limited to industrial training or made into tractable tools for the creation of wealth. He was influential in the excellent and enduring Birmingham and Midland Institute, as were many other members of the liberal Birmingham families mentioned here [47]. In his presidential address of 1867, Matthew Hill upheld the principle "Knowledge is Power" for all, and praised the great men of Birmingham such as Priestley, Boulton and Watt. His brother Frederic Hill worked hard to promote state education, a cause for which Birmingham became famous [48].

Women's Education and Emancipation

The Institute ran some very popular classes for females [49], although generally the inheritance of Priestley and the Lunar Society in Birmingham is equivocal with regard to women's education.

It was not until the 1870s that the Unitarians of Birmingham started to play a significant part in the establishment of the Edgbaston High School for Girls, for example [50]. On the other hand, the easy intellectual equality between men and women within the home experienced by the Lunar educationalists was echoed by their heirs as Thomas Ryland's memoirs make plain [51]. Some women used their better education professionally as the example of some of Priestley's descendants illustrate. His one daughter, Sarah Finch remained in the Birmingham area. Her youngest daughter Catherine ran a school for girls in Edgbaston, which Unitarian girls attended. She was reputed to be an "advanced teacher", writing out her own books for her pupils and using excellent methods of teaching particularly in geography. Her own great interests were in astronomy, which she taught through cards, pounding holes for the stars, and conchology from which she left a collection to the museum for elementary schools [52].

Other Unitarians sent their daughters to Miss Byerley's school in Warwickshire, an outstanding school run by the granddaughters of Josiah Wedgwood [53]. The limitations on what they could do with such an advanced education in the Nineteenth Century were very real although they often made more of their lives than subsequent historians have cared to show. Although there were some female pupils at Hill-Top, the thrust of the system was male-orientated and eulogised by its admirers as such. The idea for the school was Mrs Hill's, however, and all her eight children, including the two daughters, were educated similarly. One died quite young but the other, Caroline, had the same hatred of tyranny and injustice and belief in civil and religious freedom as her brothers [54]. Rowland and Matthew had asserted in *Public Education* that their educational principles could be applied to girls too as did Frederic Hill [55]. The Hill family's home was a centre of eager, cooperative, intellectual and liberal vitality in itself and Rowland Hill remembered warmly the part his capable mother played in this.

In these circles, women and men shared equally ideas, commitment and enthusiasm. Frederic Hill's wife, Martha Cowper, for example, wrote and illustrated educational books and corresponded with Maria Edgeworth before she met Frederic. In 1854 both they and Matthew Davenport Hill supported Barbara Leigh Smith and Bessie Parkes, great-granddaughter of Joseph Priestley, in a move for women's rights [56]. This was the beginning of the Women's Movement, which gradually did so much to alter perceptions of and opportunities for women.

It would be foolish to attempt to trace Priestley's influence or that of the Lunar Society too far into the Nineteenth Century. Nevertheless, in education, in science and technology, in widening the opportunities of both men and women below the upper classes, it can be seen that both had a deep and significant effect on Birmingham.

Notes

NB. All books published in London unless otherwise stated.

1   See especially J.Priestley, "Introductory Essays to Hartley's Theory of the
    Human Mind" (1790; 1st ed. 1775) in *The Theological and Miscellaneous
    Works of Joseph Priestley* (ed.) J.T. Rutt, 25 vols. (1817-31)
    [hereafter termed *Works*] vol. III, 167-96. See also R. Watts, "Joseph Priestley
    (1733-1804)", *Prospects, Thinkers on Education*, (1995, UNESCO)
    vol. XXIV, no. 3, 343-53; "Joseph Priestley and Education",
    Enlightenment and Dissent, (1983) no. 2, 83-100.

2   D. Hartley, *Observations on Man*, (New York, Delmar, 1976) I, 65.

3   Priestley, "Hartley's Theory",184.

4   J. Priestley, "The Doctrine of Philosophic Necessity Illustrated"
    (1782) *Works*, III, 521; Hartley, *Observations,* 82, II, 453.

5   J. Priestley, "Preface and Dedication to Heads of Lectures on a Course of
    Experimental Philosophy" (1794) *Works*, XXV 389; J. Priestley,
    'Philosophic Necessity', 515.

6   J. Priestley, Lectures on History and General Policy (Philadelphia, 1803),
    Works, XXIV; "The History and Present State of Electricity, with original
    experiments" (1767) *Works*, XXV; "Experimental Philosophy", 385.

7   J. Priestley, "A course of lectures on oratory and criticism" (1777);
    "The Rudiments of English Grammar" (1798) *Works*, XXIII, 257-482, 3-118.

8   Priestley, "Oratory", 259; Miscellaneous Observations relating to Education
    (1780) *Works*, XXV, 219.

9   Priestley, "History", 54-202, 463-83; *A Familiar Introduction to the Study of
    Electricity*, Johnson and Payne, 1769, 10.

10 Priestley, "Oratory", 255.

11 R.E. Schofield, *The Lunar Society of Birmingham* (Oxford, 1963); Priestley,
    "History" 5,22,313-17, 403-15, 471-5.

12 B. Simon, *The Two Nations and the Educational Structure 1780-1870* (1974),
    84-7; Priestley, "Miscellaneous Observations", 185-95, 206-18;
    "History",11; "Electricity", 345.

13 Priestley, "Experimental Philosophy", 389;
    "Miscellaneous Observations", 5-228.

14 Priestley, "A particular Attention to the Instruction of the Young ... Gravel-Pit
    Meeting in Hackney" December 4th, 1791, *Works*, iv-ix and Preface; J. Uglow,
    The Lunar Men (2001), 319-20, 406-7.

15 Simon, *Two Nations*, 17-71.

16 Uglow, *Lunar Men*, 257, passim.

17 J. Priestley, "The Proper Objects of Education in the present State of the
    World...", (1791) *Works*, XV, 431, 434-5.

18 Julia Wedgwood, *The Personal Life of Josiah Wedgwood the Potter,* 2 vols.
    (Manchester, 1915), II, 433, 547- 548, 555-6;
    Henrietta Litchfield (ed.), *Emma Darwin. A Century of Family Letters 1792-
    1896,* 2 vols. (1915), I, 61-2.
19 E. Darwin, *The Botanic Garden,* (1795) canto 1, 84-90,
    note XXII, 53-9 and passim.
20 See examples at Soho House.
21 Priestley, "Miscellaneous Observations", 185-95, 206-18, passim;
    "History", 5,22,311-17,403-15,471-5; "Electricity", 345;
    "Experimental philosophy", 389; "Proper objects", 420-1;
    Autobiography of ..., (Bath, 1970; 1st ed. 1806), 88-9.
22 Maria & R. L. Edgeworth, *Practical Education* 3 vols. (1801),
    I, pp. 179, 258-60, 272-3, 258; III, pp. 1-26, 48, 53-5, 229, 272, 279-80,
    300, 311, 325-57.
23 Erasmus Darwin, *A Plan for the Conduct of Female Education in Boarding
    Schools* (Derby, 1797), passim.
24 Christina C. Hankin (ed.),
    The Life of Mary Anne Schimmelpenninck (1858), passim.
25 William Matthews, *A Sketch of the Principal Means which have been
    employed to ameliorate the Intellectual and Moral Condition of the
    Working-Classes in Birmingham* (1830), 6-14.
26 *Ibid.,* 14-18, 22-5.
27 William Henry Ryland (ed.), *Reminiscences of Thomas Henry Ryland*
    (Birmingham, 1904), pp. 64-70.
28 Matthews, *Birmingham,* 23-4.
29 *Ibid.,* 5-15; Emily Bushrod, *The History of Unitarianism in Birmingham
    from the middle of the Eighteenth Century to 1893,* Unpublished MA,
    University of Birmingham, 1954, 206-17, passim; T.W. Hill, *Course of
    Evening's Instructions for a Limited Number of Persons* (Birmingham,
    1804).
30 Rowland & George Birkbeck Hill, *The Life of Sir Rowland Hill* (1880),
    7-16; Rosamund & Florence Davenport Hill, *The Recorder of Birmingham.
    A Memoir of Matthew Davenport Hill* (1878), 1-6; Constance Hill (ed.),
    Frederic Hill. An Autobiography of Fifty Years in Times of Reform (1894),
    7-8, 17-23.
31 R. & G.B. Hill, *Rowland Hill,* 19-34, 52ff., 142; R. & F. D. Hill, *Recorder,* 7-13.
32 W. H. G. Armytage, "The Lunar Society and its Contribution to Education",
    University of Birmingham Historical Journal, (1967-8) V, 67.
33 M. D. Hill & Rowland Hill, *Plans for the Government and Liberal Instruction
    of Boys in Large Numbers Drawn from Experience [Public Education]* (1822),

121-2, viii, 105, 128, 192, 199, 204 ftn; R. & G. B. Hill, *Rowland Hill*, 49-50, 160-8; C. Hill, *Frederic Hill*, 26-7.

34 Elie Halevy, *The Growth of Philosophic Radicalism* (1972) Faber, pp.153-4, 249-478, 433, 491.

35 M.D. & R. Hill, *Public Education,* passim.

36 Maria & R. L. Edgeworth, *Practical Education*; Watts, "Joseph Priestley", 343-53; "Joseph Priestley and Education", 83-100.

37 M.D. & R. Hill, *Public Education,* passim; R. & G.B. Hill, *Rowland Hill,* pp. 91- 9.

38 Brayley, *Knowledge of Nature*, passim.

39 *Hazelwood Magazine* I, No. I, pp. 3-5; No. 13, pp.1, 5.

40 M.D. & R. Hill, *Public Education,* passim.

41 Ibid., passim; Jeremy Bentham, *Chrestomathia* (1816), passim; *Westminster Review* (1824), 1, pp.75-9.

42 P. W. J. Bartrip, "A Thoroughly Good School", *British Journal of Educational Studies,* (1980) XXVIII, 49-59; William Henry Ryland (ed.), *Reminiscences of Thomas Henry Ryland* (Birmingham, 1904), pp. 24-8, 77-8.

43 R. & G. B. Hill, *Rowland Hill*, 66.

44 Ibid., I, pp. 184-98, 207-14 & passim; Colin C. Hey, *Rowland Hill: Genius and Benefactor 1795-1879,* (1989) 25-43, 175-6,passim.

45 Eg see Ryland, *Reminiscences*, 25-6, 69-70, 102-6 & passim.

46 Ibid., 79-80; Herbart New, *Centenary of the Church of the Messiah (formerly New Street) Sunday Schools* (Birmingham, 1888), 14-20; *Monthly Repository* (1831), New Series 5, pp. 68-72 (article sent in by Rev John Kentish, minister at the New Meeting); Matthews, *Sketch*, pp. 29-33; Hey, *Rowland Hill*, 103-9, passim; Brian Simon, *Two Nations*, 116.

47 R.& F.D. Hill, *Recorder of Birmingham*, 163, 170-1, 254-5; Conrad Gill, *A History of Birmingham* 2 vols. (Oxford, 1952), I, p. 394-5; Arthur Godloe , "The Birmingham Midland Institute" in J.H. Muirhead (ed.), *Birmingham Institutions* (Birmingham, 1911), 317-62.

48 Matthew Davenport Hill, *Address delivered at the Birmingham and Midland Institute* (1867), pp. 5-9, 17-25; Frederic Hill, *National Education* 2 vols. (1836).

49 Ryland, *Reminiscences*, 135-43, 147; *Birmingham and Midland Institute Reports* (Birmingham 1857-61), 1856, pp. 3-5,7; 1859, pp. 4,7; 1860, p. 9.

50 Janet Whitcut, *Edgbaston High School,* (Birmingham,1976), 1-67.

51 Ryland, *Reminiscences*, passim.

52 Ronald Martineau Dixon, "Priestley's Daughter and her Descendants", *TUHS* (1931-4), V. pp.43-66, 288-93, 411-16; Norah Byng Kenrick (ed.), *Chronicles of a Nonconformist Family. The Kenricks of Wynne Hall, Exeter and Birmingham* (Birmingham, 1932), 145.

53 *Ibid.*, 161-5, 217; Phyllis D. Hicks, *A Quest of Ladies. The Story of a Warwickshire School* (Birmingham, 1949), passim; *DNB,* 'John Kenrick', XXXI, 14-16.

54 Hey, *Rowland Hill,* 43 & passim; R. Hill, *Rowland Hill,* 30, 47, 152-5, 193-5; Ryland *Reminiscences,* 24, 71, 79, 85, 101-2, 129, 131, 133, 139.

55 R. & M.D. Hill, *Public Education,* p.vii; F. Hill, *National Education* I, pp. 204 - 14.

56 R. and F.D. Hill, *Recorder of Birmingham* , 114-5; C. Hill, *Frederic Hill,* 77, 92-9, 188-93, 233, 305-9; R. Hill, *Rowland Hill,* 19-30, 47, 82, 142, 184-98; Dixon, 'Priestley's Daughter', 53-4.

Chapter 7

JOSEPH PRIESTLEY,
THE LUNAR SOCIETY AND ANTI-SLAVERY

Malcolm Dick

Joseph Priestley was a man of wide cultural sympathies. He could read Arabic, Chaldee, French, German, Greek, Hebrew, Italian, Latin and Syriac [1]. The inventory of his books in Birmingham City Archives shows that he owned a number of classical, theological and scientific works, a Hebrew Bible, books describing voyages to Africa, the West Indies and Japan and oriental tales, including volumes of Persian stories and the Arabian Nights [2]. One of his friends was the liberal Catholic priest, theologian and historian, Joseph Berington (1743-1827) who was based at Oscott, near Birmingham in the 1780s, and to whom he dedicated one of his publications [3]. Priestley also proposed a dialogue with Jewish people, a particularly despised group in late Eighteenth-Century society.

Portrait of Joseph Priestley. Local Studies and History, Birmingham Central Library.

He hoped that God would put an end to the sufferings of "the most despised, of all nations of the earth" [4]. As a Unitarian, Priestley was also a member of a nonconformist minority which faced discrimination because he did not conform to the teachings of the Church of England [5]. His religious experiences, humanitarian sentiments and understanding of different cultures predisposed him to address Black slavery, which he described as "perhaps the greatest, and most crying evil under the sun" [6].

This article explores Priestley's contribution to the anti-slavery campaign in the West Midlands during the late Eighteenth Century. It locates Priestley in the context of an abolitionist culture in the 1770s and 1780s to which many of his colleagues in the Lunar Society also contributed. It argues that Priestley provided a sophisticated attack on both slavery and the slave trade by addressing philosophical, psychological and economic arguments as well as appealing to the humanitarian sentiments and empathy of his audience. The paper also notes that anti-slavery principles were compromised by economic and social considerations. Priestley may not have been immune from compromising his own beliefs during the final years of his life in the slave-owning society of the United States.

The Context

Britain was the most significant slave-trading nation by the late Eighteenth Century and its market for sugar sustained Atlantic slavery. Black slaves from Africa were transported to the Caribbean and America to work on plantations producing sugar in the West Indies and cotton, rice and tobacco on the mainland. The slave system depended on two things: an adequate supply of labour and a buoyant market for the crops that slaves produced and processed. British consumption of sugar increased ten-fold between 1700 and 1800 and the country consumed more sugar than the rest of Europe combined. Most slave economies in the West Indies failed to reproduce themselves, so plantation owners argued that the slave trade was essential to enable demand for produce to be satisfied and maintain their profits. Ports such as Liverpool and Bristol depended on the trade for their prosperity and further inland Birmingham's manufacturers profited from the guns that were exchanged for slaves and the shackles and chains that restrained them[7].

"Am I not a man and a Brother?" Print of Josiah Wedgwood's design for the anti-slavery campaign to illustrate Erasmus Darwin's poem, The Botanic Garden (London, 1791). Arts, Languages and Literature, Birmingham Central Library.

The anti-slavery movement had its origins in the efforts of individuals who were shocked by the cruelty of the slave trade and the inhuman treatment of slaves. They included Quakers and other Christians such as Granville Sharp, Thomas Clarkson, John Newton and William Wilberforce. One early success of the abolitionists was the judgement of Lord Mansfield, the Lord Chief Justice in 1772, which declared that under English law, "the claim of slavery can never be supported". This meant that slavery was illegal in England, but it had no effect on the slave trade or slavery in the West Indies. In 1787 a committee was formed in London to demand an end to the trade. It formed the nucleus of a campaign which attracted supporters from all social classes. By 1791 the campaign had secured the signatures of 400,000 people on more than 500 petitions against the trade [8].

The Midlands was an important location for the attack on slavery and important roles were played by individuals who were connected through the Lunar Society, such as Thomas Day, Josiah Wedgwood, Erasmus Darwin and Joseph Priestley. The Lunar Society was composed of industrialists, scientists, inventors and philosophers who met at the time of the full moon between the 1760s and early 1800s in the English West Midlands. They are best-known for their contributions to the steam engine, factory production and canal development, but they also contributed to progressive political and social causes such as education and anti-slavery. The most extensive discussion of their approach to anti-slavery is contained in Jenny Uglow's book, *The Lunar Men* [9]. Biographies of Erasmus Darwin by Desmond King-Hele, Josiah Wedgwood by Robin Reilly and Thomas Day by Peter Rowland also draw attention to the anti-slavery commitments of these individuals. The Boulton and Watt Archives in Birmingham City Archives provide an insight into the ambiguous approaches of these two leading industrialists. Samuel Galton junior, a Quaker who ostensibly was a pacifist and opponent of slavery, justified his sale of guns to Africa as part of the slave trade [10]. The approach of Joseph Priestley to anti-slavery is largely ignored by those who have chronicled his life. Priestley's biographers have concentrated on his theology, science or politics, to the neglect of his interest in social issues.

Writing in the late Nineteenth-Century, J. A. Langford in *A Century of Birmingham Life* traced the origins of anti-slavery in the town to a visit by Thomas Clarkson, the campaigner against slavery, in 1787. Clarkson's visit acted as a catalyst and he singled out local Quakers such as Sampson and Charles Lloyd and the Unitarian William Russell as especially supportive, but this was not the only factor [11]. In 1773, Thomas Day, who periodically resided in Lichfield and frequently visited his Lunar friends in Birmingham, wrote *The Dying Negro*, a poem denouncing slavery. Written in the first person, the poem contrasted the feelings of a dying slave with a devastating attack on slavery. The poem sold well and Day prepared a second edition in 1774 when Britain was stumbling into war with America. The American colonists sought the pursuit of liberty, but as slave owners, he claimed, they denied freedom to slaves. In the preface to the poem, Day noted: "For them the Negro is dragged from his cottage, and his plantane shade…the rights of nature are invaded; and European faith becomes infamous throughout the globe…These are the men whose clamours for liberty and independence are heard across the Atlantic Ocean!" Day could not stand hypocrisy. In 1784, he published his *Fragment of an original letter on the slavery of Negroes* which berated the Americans further: "If there be an object truly ridiculous in nature, it is an American patriot signing resolutions of independence with one hand, and with the other brandishing a whip over his affrighted slaves" [12].

Other local figures were also prominent campaigners. In 1787, Day's colleague in the Lunar Society, Josiah Wedgwood, commissioned a design for the Society for the Suppression of the Slave Trade. The image depicted a kneeling slave in chains, the outer edge modelled with the words "AM I NOT A MAN AND A BROTHER?" It became the symbol of the abolitionist campaign and appeared as cameos on brooches, buttons and snuff boxes. Wedgwood led the anti-slave trade petitioning campaign in North Staffordshire and corresponded with James Watt on the issue [13].

A third Lunar Society figure who attacked slavery was Dr Erasmus Darwin. In 1789 Darwin corresponded with Wedgwood on the matter: "I have just heard that there are muzzles or gags made in Birmingham for the slaves in our islands. If this be true, and such an instrument could be exhibited by a speaker in the house of commons, it might have a great effect"[14]. Darwin also produced attacks on slavery in his poetry. In *The Loves of the Plants,* published anonymously in April 1789, he called on MPs to abolish slavery and in *The Economy of Vegetation*, published in June 1791, he attacked Britain's economic exploitation of Africans:

Hear, oh, BRITANNIA! Potent Queen of isles,
On whom fair Art and meek Religion smiles,
How AFRIC'S coasts thy craftier sons invade
With murder, rapine, theft, - and call it Trade!
- The SLAVE, in chains, on supplicating knee,
Spreads his wide arms, and lifts his eyes to Thee;
With hunger pale, with wounds and toil oppress'd,
"ARE WE NOT BRETHREN?" sorrow chokes the rest;-

Darwin's use of the phrase "Are we not Brethren?" refers to Wedgwood's design for the anti-slavery campaign. He selected the image to illustrate *The Botanic Garden* which became the collective title to contain these two poems [15].

Priestley and the local anti-slavery campaign

When Priestley entered the campaign in 1788, he was already part of a regional anti-slavery culture to which Day, Wedgwood and Darwin had contributed. In January 1788, a local committee was formed in Birmingham to secure parliamentary approval to abolish the slave trade. According to a notice in *Aris's*

Birmingham Gazette in that month, two local Anglican clerics, Charles Curtis, Rector of St Martin's and Spencer Madan, Rector of St Philip's were chosen to correspond with Parliament to end this "Disgrace to Europe" and "violation of Christian Law". The local campaign crossed the nonconformist versus Anglican divide in Birmingham as Priestley, who was also a member of the committee, noted. Writing to Rev Mr Emans in Coventry, Priestley announced:

> *Being one of the Committee of correspondence for an application to Parliament for the abolition of the slave trade, I take the liberty to send you copies of such tracts as are available for the purpose. We shall have a petition from Birmingham, and hope to be joined by one from Coventry, and in promoting this I depend upon your active concurrence. You will see by the names of our Committee, that there is no party business with us. Our meetings are perfectly harmonious, and will tend, I hope, to lessen much of that bigotry, by which this town has been distinguished* [16].

On 23rd January 1788, he delivered a sermon in Birmingham against the slave trade, which he published the following month. Described by Langford, as "an eloquent and forcible discourse", the sermon delivered a battery of statements against slavery and the slave trade. Priestley took as his text a quotation from the *Acts of the Apostles*: "And hath made of one Blood all Nations of Men to dwell on all the face of the earth" [17]. He used this Biblical message to launch a range of moral, philosophical and practical arguments attacking the treatment of his fellow human beings.

Like many other campaigners, Priestley's case focused on the psychological and physical cruelty of the slave trade and slavery, but he also produced theoretical arguments underlying the distinctive humanity and philosophy of his approach. Priestley's theology was optimistic. He believed that God would ensure that good would ultimately triumph and slavery would be abolished. It is "the intention of Providence finally to exterminate all evil." This did not mean, however, that human beings should passively await the end of wickedness: "we may, and ought, as

Woman losing her children as a result of the slave trade. Records of the Female Society for the Relief of British Negro Slaves, Birmingham City Archives.

his own children, to act like God; exerting ourselves, by every means in our power, to remove the prejudices, correct the errors, cure the vices, and relieve the distresses, of our fellow creatures" [18]. This required recognising the shared humanity which crossed racial and religious barriers:

> *You will consider all mankind as brethren, and neighbours...As men, and as Christians...we should not rest ourselves not only for our relations...or friends; not only for our countrymen; not only for Europeans, but for the different inhabitants of Asia, Africa or America; and not only for Christians but for Jews, Mahometans, and Infidels. And as we ought to feel for our fellow men we ought, to the utmost extent of our influence, to exert ourselves to relieve their distresses* [19].

Slavery, Priestley claimed, was the greatest evil that society had to address [20]. He had to justify this contention and argue for the abolition of both slavery and the slave trade which sustained it.

Firstly, slavery and the slave trade inflicted mental and physical suffering. There was psychological cruelty:

> *I have been informed by a person who resided in Jamaica, that it is usual for the slaves, after they are purchased, to shudder at the sight of a fire, or kitchen utensils, imagining that they are to be killed and eaten, till older slaves convince them that nothing of that kind is intended. What the poor creatures must suffer with this idea on their minds all the voyage, and the terror it must impress on the country in general, in which thousands who are never taken know they are liable to it, is not to be estimated, and for which no good treatment of slaves can compensate* [21].

The trade, moreover, degraded women and destroyed families. Women were subjected to "shocking indecencies … during the voyage, and afterwards". Friends, relations, husbands, wives and children were separated "both when they are put on board the ships, and at the place of sale" [22]. The slave trade also resulted in the multiple killing of human beings before they even started work:

> *In order to raise our sugar, and other West-India commodities, perhaps half a million of persons are annually destroyed, and in a manner peculiarly shocking to humanity. To die by an earthquake, by pestilence, or even by famine, would be merciful compared with the manner in which these poor wretches often perish. All the European plantations taken together are said to require an annual supply of sixty thousand fresh slaves; but these are those that remain after so many have died in what is called the seasoning, before they can be*

brought to bear the labour to which they are made to submit; and after so many more have been lost during the voyage, owing to their mode of confinement, and ill usage on board, that it is said not less than a hundred thousand are annually exported from Africa. And some say that before this ten are destroyed for one that is secured, and safely lodged on board the ships[23].

Secondly, the cruelty, degradation and destruction of slavery could not be prevented by acts of humane treatment by their masters. Slavery itself was an exploitative relationship between owners and slaves. The latter were subjected to the arbitrary will of others: "Under humane masters, slaves may, no doubt, enjoy a certain degree of happiness; but still they are slaves, subject to the wills, and consequently the caprices, of others; and there is no proper security from the greatest outrages, but in the protection of *law*"[24]. Slavery, though, was an abuse of power: "In general, it is said, that in our plantations slaves

The mode of flogging Slaves. Records of the Female Society for the Relief of British Negro Slaves, Birmingham City Archives.

are employed so many hours every day, excepting Sundays, in the service of their masters, that they have only one for themselves, and but little sleep. For remissness in labour they are severely beaten, and for rebellion (as any attempt to recover their liberty is called) they are generally gibetted alive"[25].

Thirdly, the English in particular should be ashamed of their involvement in the institution. "No Europeans" he argued, used their slaves "with so much cruelty as the English." Compared to the French and the Spanish governments, which provided regulations and codes of laws to protect their slaves, those "belonging to the English are almost wholly left to the mercy of their masters; and the annual consumption of them is itself proof of the most cruel usage"[26]. These masters, moreover, were dehumanised by their ability to exercise arbitrary power: "Such a power as that which a master exercises over a slave necessarily tends to make him haughty, cruel, and capricious, unfit for the society of his equals, which is the happiest state of man"[27]. This was a particularly incendiary argument to use in Birmingham, given that many people benefited from the local production of chains, shackles and guns which were to enslave Africans as part of the slave trade.

Fourthly, economic arguments which might be used to justify slavery were weak. Priestley took exception to the argument that the slave trade could not be abandoned because it was "a valuable source of national profit...." Such a trade was "*wicked* and *unlawful*, such as no advantage can justify." Religion and morality dictated that "a Christian nation should not hesitate to do what is right in itself." Moreover, abolishing slavery itself was likely to be economically beneficial. "End the expensive plantation system and enable the African economies to develop with free labour", he claimed. Priestley also argued that the Quaker masters who freed their chattels and employed them as paid labourers, found that they did more work as freemen than as slaves [28].

Fifthly, it was wrong to justify slavery on the grounds that Africans were inferior to Europeans. Priestley recognised the equality of all human beings whatever their colour. Africans were human beings with the same capacity for reflection, pain and achievement. Man had "the power of reflexion in an eminent degree; and it is this that makes him miserable in a state of servitude." This "agony of mind" led "great numbers of Negroes" to "put an end

The separation of a family of slaves.... Records of the Female Society for the Relief of British Negro Slaves, Birmingham City Archives.

Slaves exposed for Sale. Records of the Female Society for the Relief of British Negro Slaves, Birmingham City Archives.

to their own lives." Their torment would not end until they were dehumanised by their experience: "And they will be incapable of any degree of happiness in a state of servitude, till their feelings are blunted, and they are reduced to a condition nearly approaching that of the brutes" [29]. Moreover, Priestley argued that Africans were not culturally or intellectually inferior to Europeans:

Some Europeans, finding Negro slaves in this wretched degraded condition, to which they themselves have reduced them, have had the assurance, and the folly, to pronounce them to be a species of men greatly inferior to themselves. But were the Europeans treated in the same manner a sufficient length of time, it is demonstrable that the most intelligent of them would be no better. Those who see Negroes in their native country, or in circumstances of better treatment among ourselves, are satisfied that they are by no means inferior to Europeans in point of understanding. According to the observations of a late ingenious traveller, the ancient Egyptians so famed for their wisdom, were the very same people with the present Negroes [31].

Humanity was indivisible. All people whatever their race, belief or background could suffer, think and participate in creating civilisation.

Principles into Practice

Principles had to be translated into practice. On 11th February, 1788, a local meeting was held which resulted in the construction of a petition to Parliament from the inhabitants of Birmingham and its neighbourhood seeking "a total ABOLITION" of the slave trade. Money was also raised to support national anti-slave trade activity. The local campaign faced opposition. One result was a published pamphlet: *A proposal for the Consideration of those who interest themselves in the Abolition or Prevention of the Slave Trade* and letters to *Aris's Gazette* in 1788 and 1789 which called for regulation rather than abolition. The tone of the pamphlet and letters suggest that the opponents of the petitioners were on the defensive in the face of activity which commanded the support of Anglican and nonconformist leaders such as Curtis, Madan, Priestley and prominent secular figures such as

Portrait of Olaudah Equiano, the frontispiece to The Interesting Narrative of the Life of Olaudah Equiano or Gustavus Vassa, the African (London, Sixth Edition, 1793). Local Studies and History, Birmingham Central Library.

Charles Lloyd, Samuel Garbett, William Russell, Francis Perrott and William Villiers. In February 1790, the local focus shifted to Parliament when William Wilberforce MP secured the creation of a House of Commons Committee to examine witnesses on behalf of abolition and on 18th April 1791 he introduced a motion to abolish the trade. The bill failed to secure majority support in the House of Commons but local abolitionists continued their abolitionist activities [31].

At least two approaches were pursued. One was educational, which involved acquiring more information about the experience of slavery and the slave trade, securing publicity for the cause and solidifying local commitment to the campaign. The autobiography of a former slave, Olaudah Equiano, provided a means of achieving these ends. Equiano or Gustavus Vasa, as he was known by his Christian name, was the most prominent Black British campaigner against slavery. He had been sold into slavery as a boy, but a master had provided him with education and Equiano had subsequently purchased his freedom. He became a successful businessman and his best-selling autobiography provided a vivid account of his experiences before, during and after slavery. Equiano promoted his book via national tours and he came to Birmingham. *Aris's Birmingham Gazette* of June 28, 1790 notes that Matthew Boulton, Samuel Galton (presumably the elder) and Joseph Priestley, alongside other prominent local people, were subscribers to Equiano's, *Interesting Narrative*. Equiano's letter thanking his supporters in Birmingham for their "Acts of Kindness and Hospitality" was published in *Aris's Gazette* [32].

A second approach was through economic pressure. A boycott of West Indian sugar was designed to attack the economic basis of slavery. A voluntary ban on sugar had been suggested in pamphlets in the 1780s. One author, William Fox argued that the slave trade would end if 38,000 families boycotted West Indian sugar. By the 1780s, Britain consumed more sugar than the rest of Europe combined, so the anti-saccharists had considerable potential to make an impact. On one of his tours in 1791, Thomas Clarkson noted:

There was no town, through which I passed, in which there was not one individual who had left off the use of sugar....They were of all ranks and parties. Rich and poor, churchmen and dissenters had adopted this measure....in gentlemen's families, where the master had set the example, the servants had often voluntarily followed it; and even children...excluded with the most virtuous resolution, the sweets...from their lips [33].

An insight into motives is provided by the young Mary Anne Galton, the daughter of Lunar Society member Samuel Galton junior:

My father had a very large acquaintance with the affluent West India merchants of Liverpool. They were most kindly, generous, and hospitable; their houses were like palaces. I was amazed to see the sumptuous drawing-rooms, rich with satin and silk, in houses where there was no library. But what surprised me most...was the multitude of black servants, almost all of whom had originally been slaves; this deeply moved my compassion, and when I saw the table laden with West India produce, in its various forms of fruit and sweetmeats, and saw the black servants looking on at the produce of a land, their native home, which they had left for us, and of which they might not partake, my heart often ached; and it is no wonder that my resolution was confirmed never to taste anything made with sugar, or to use other West Indian commodities [34].*

Thousands of people stopped consuming sugar or substituted East Indian sugar for the West Indian version. One report showed that a Birmingham grocer found that his sugar sales were cut by 50% in four months. Despite widespread support, the Anti-saccharist campaign failed to change the law. There is no evidence that Joseph Priestley supported this aspect of the anti-slavery campaign. During the second half of 1791, he faced more immediate priorities following the destruction of his property during the Priestley Riots.

Compromises

The anti-slavery campaign was a contested one, marked by compromise and the dissolving of principle in the face of economic or social pressures. Two Lunar Society figures, Matthew Boulton and James Watt were industrialists who were willing to do business with West Indian slave owners. They explored the prospect of selling steam engines to slave plantations in the Caribbean and in 1783 Boulton entertained Mr Pennant, a notorious slave owner who owned huge estates in Jamaica and sought steam engines for his plantations there. In 1790 Samuel Galton recommended to John Dawson, a Liverpool-based slave trader, that he should contact Boulton and Watt about supplying steam engines for Dawson's sugar works in Trinidad. The latter wrote to Boulton and Watt on 9th November 1790. Boulton and Watt's reply to Dawson does not survive, but their partnership supplied steam engines to plantations in the West Indies at later dates.

Watt, nevertheless, was a critic of slavery. On 31st October 1791, he corresponded on behalf of the firm of Boulton and Watt to Messrs Beguye & Co. of Nantes concerning the suspension of the production of their steam engine order following the outbreak of the slave revolt in the French West Indian colony of San Domingo (now Haiti). Watt wrote: "...we heartily pray that the system of slavery so disgraceful to humanity were abolished by prudent though progressive measures" [35].

The role of another Lunar Society figure and Birmingham manufacturer, Samuel Galton junior, reveals the compromises which one businessman made when his interests conflicted with principle. Galton was a Quaker, a member of the Society of Friends and therefore a member of a pacifist sect, and the family firm made huge sums of money exporting guns which were sold as part of the slave trade. Galton was forced by his fellow Quakers after 1792 to confront the tensions between his beliefs and his business interests. His father, Samuel Galton senior retired from the gun trade, but Samuel Galton junior continued as a weapons manufacturer. He mounted a spirited defence in *To the Friends of the Monthly Meeting at Birmingham*, 1795:

> *The censure and the laws of the Society against slavery are as strict and decisive as against war. Now, those who use the produce of the labour of slaves, such as Tobacco, Rum, Sugar, Rice, Indigo and Cotton, are more intimately and directly the promoters of the slave trade, than the vendor of arms is the promoter of war, because the consumption of these articles is the very ground and cause of slavery.*

These arguments did not carry weight with the Society of Friends and on 10th August 1796 it disowned Samuel Galton junior as a member. Galton continued to attend Quaker worship but could no longer participate in business meetings. When he gave up the gun business in 1804 and started banking, the Society accepted a donation from him towards the enlargement of the Quaker burial ground. The historian Barbara M D Smith records: "Galton's attitude reflects an entrepreneur's pragmatic approach to moral issues that conflict with business and a robust determination to speak out plainly..." [36]

The 1790s and early 1800s were difficult years for the anti-slavery campaign. The French Revolution changed the political climate. The terror, execution of the King Louis XVI and the outbreak of war between

Portrait of Matthew Boulton. Local Studies and History, Birmingham Central Library.

Britain and France in 1793 meant that abolitionism, with its emphasis on human rights, could easily be linked with demands for political radicalism and support for an enemy state. Campaigners seemed to be dangerous and unpatriotic. The Priestley Riots of July 1791 weakened the campaign in the West Midlands. Priestley, the philosopher of anti-slavery and political liberty, was forced to flee Birmingham after the destruction of his house, books and laboratory. He moved to London and, in 1794, he departed for the United States. In Northumberland, Pennsylvania, Priestley lived in a society where slavery was legal. The Priestley household employed hired slaves as servants. To what extent this affected Priestley's conscience as an advocate of anti-slavery remains unclear [37].

Abolition

The anti-slavery campaigners continued to press for change, focusing on the abolition of the slave trade, rather than the abolition of slavery, as the measure that was most likely to gain support in Parliament. They included political conservatives like William Wilberforce MP and Prime Minister William Pitt. In opposition to the economic interests of many within their social class, the abolition of the British slave trade was secured in 1807. Slavery remained intact, but many abolitionists hoped that it would wither away once the plantation system was deprived of its injection of new slaves from Africa. This did not happen quickly. In the 1820s the campaign revived, focusing on the removal of slavery itself. Once again activists in the West Midlands were prominent, including members of *The Female Society for the Relief of British Negro Slaves* which was founded in 1825. Amongst the supporters were descendants of the Lunar men. Members of the Committee included Mrs Moilliet, the daughter of James Keir, Miss Galton, Mrs Schimmelpenninck (Mary Anne Galton), Mrs Sneyd Edgeworth and Miss Wedgwood. The Society aimed to encourage a "lively sense of the injustice, inhumanity and impiety of our present system of Colonial Slavery" and used its financial resources to support campaigning activities. Amongst other things it reproduced prints and republished newspaper articles drawing attention to its evils of slavery. Joseph Sturge, a Birmingham businessman, was also an important abolitionist, becoming Secretary of the local Anti-slavery Society in 1826. Sturge's impact was most apparent after 1836 when he visited the Caribbean and campaigned for improved labour conditions, after the abolition of slavery in 1833 [38]. Joseph Priestley died before the slave trade and slavery were abolished, but as a theorist and activist he was an important contributor to the abolitionist campaign between 1788 and 1790. His *Sermon* of 1788 focused on the common humanity and shared experiences which united all human beings despite differences in colour, race and creed.

Notes

1 Gibbs, F W, *Joseph Priestley: Adventurer in Science and Champion of Truth* (London, Nelson, 1965), pp. 4-7.

2 Inventory of the House of Priestley and Books of Dr Joseph Priestley which were destroyed during the riots at Birmingham in 1791. Birmingham City Archives (BCA) 3999801/IIR 30.

3 "Dedication to the Reverend Joseph Berrington (sic)…" in Priestley Collection by Samuel Timmins. BCA. IIR10 73499. There are references to Berington in Hankin, Christiana C. (ed.), Life of Mary Anne Schimmelpenninck
(Mary Anne Galton), London, Longman, third edition,1860).
A brief biography of Berington can be found in
http://www.newadvent.org/cathen/02491a.htm

4 *Letters to the Jews; inviting them to an amicable discussion of the evidences of Christianity*, Second Edition,
(Birmingham, Printed for the author by Pearson and Rollason;
and sold by J Johnson, No 72, St Paul's Churchyard, London, 1787).

5 See Hill, Gay, "Gunpowder Joe: Priestley's Religious Radicalism" in this volume.

6 Priestley, Joseph, *A Sermon on the Subject of the Slave Trade; Delivered to a Society of Protestant Dissenters, at the New Meeting in Birmingham; and published at their Request*
(Birmingham, printed for the Author, by Pearson and Rollason, 1788), p. 23.

7 Many books explore the history of the slave trade and the abolitionist movement in the late Eighteenth Century. See, for example, Anstey, Roger, *The Atlantic Slave Trade and British Abolition, 1760-1810* (London, MacMillan, 1975); Walvin, James, *Black Ivory: A History of British Slavery* (London, Harper Collins, 1992); Walvin, James, "British Abolitionism 1787-1838" in Tibbles, Anthony (ed.), *Transatlantic Slavery: Against Human Dignity* (London, HMSO, National Museums and Galleries on Merseyside, 1994), pp. 87-95; Blackburn, Robin, *The Overthrow of Colonial Slavery 1776-1848* (London, Verso, 1988); Grosvenor, Ian, Roberts, Sian and Tait, Fiona, "Making Connections: Birmingham, West Africa, West Indies and the Indian sub-continent in the eighteenth and nineteenth centuries" in Grosvenor, Ian, Mclean, Rita and Roberts, *Making Connections: Birmingham Black International History*
(Birmingham, Black Pasts, Birmingham Futures Group, 2002), pp. 45-49.

8 See note 7 above.

9 Uglow, Jenny, *The Lunar Men: The Friends who made the Future* (London, Faber and Faber, 2002), pp. 258-62, 410-14.

10 Guyatt, Mary, "The Wedgwood Slave Medallion: Values in Eighteenth-Century Design", Journal of Design History, Vol 13, No 2, 2000; King-Hele, Desmond, *Erasmus Darwin: A Life of Unequalled Achievement* (London, Giles de la Mare, 1999), pp. 115, 231-2, 240, 262, 303, 309; Reilly, Robin, *Josiah Wedgwood, 1730-1795* (London, Macmillan, 1992), pp. 284-89; Rowland, Peter, *The Life and Times of Thomas Day, 1784-1789: English Philanthropist and Author. Virtue Almost Personified* (Lewiston/ Queenstown/ Lampeter, The Edwin Mellen Press, 1996), pp. 55-58, 79-87, Appendix A; Smith, Barbara M. D., "The Galtons of Birmingham: Quaker Gun Merchants and Bankers, 1702-1831", *Business History*, vol. ix, no 2 July 1967. p. 147.

11 Langford, J.A, *A Century of Birmingham Life: or, a Chronicle of Local Events, from 1741 to 1841* (Birmingham, W G Moore and Co., 1870), Vol. 1, p. 434-435; The Lloyd family had contributed to the creation of the national anti-slavery campaign see Lloyd, Humphrey, *The Quaker Lloyds in the Industrial Revolution* (London, Hutchinson, 1975), pp. 199-203. Russell had been instrumental in securing Priestley's appointment to the New Meeting in Birmingham. For Russell see Mason, Shena, "Friends Reunited: Dr Priestley and the Russells of Birmingham" in this publication.

12 Rowland, op.cit., pp. 55-58, 79-87.

13 Josiah Wedgwood to James Watt, 14th February 1788: "I take it for granted that you & I are on the same side of the question respecting the slave trade. I have joined my brethren here in a petition from the pottery for the *abolition* of it, as I do not like a half measure in this *black business.*"
BCA. James Watt Papers. 6/272 20.

14 Erasmus Darwin to Josiah Wedgwood, 13th April 1789.
Darwin Archive at Cambridge University Library. 227.1:112.
Quoted in King-Hele, *op.cit.*, p. 232.

15 *Ibid.*, pp. 231-32.

16 Joseph Priestley to the Rev Mr Emans, 13th January 1788. Priestley Collection by Samuel Timmins. BCA. IIR10 73499.

17 Langford, op. cit., p. 435.

18 Priestley, Joseph, *A Sermon on the Subject of the Slave Trade...op.cit.*, p. v.

19 *Ibid.*, p. 1-2.

20 *Ibid.*, p. 23.

21 *Ibid.*, p. xii.

22 *Ibid.*, p. 6.

23 *Ibid.*, p. 5-6.

24 *Ibid.*, p. xi.

25 *Ibid.*, p. 7-8.

26 *Ibid.*, p. 8-9.

27 *Ibid.*, p. 21.

28 *Ibid.*, p. 25-29.

29 *Ibid.*, p. 9.

30 *Ibid.*, p. 20.

31 Langford, *op. cit.*, pp. 436-41.

32 Equiano, Olaudah, *The Interesting Narrative of the Life of Olaudah Equiano or Gustavus Vasa, the African,* (London, Sixth edition, 1793); Caretta, Vincent (ed.), *Olaudah Equiano's Interesting Narrative and Other Writings* (Penguin, 1995); Aris's Birmingham Gazette, 24th December 1789, 19th June 1790.

33 Clarkson, Thomas, *The History of the ...Abolition of the African Slave Trade...vol II.*
(London, Frank Cass, reprint of 1808 edition, 1968), pp. 347-250.

34 Hankin, Christiana C. (ed.), *op.cit.*, pp. 243-244.

35 Loggie, Val, McArdle, Jane and McLean, Rita, "Soho House and Matthew Boulton; making new connections" in Grosvenor, Mclean and Roberts, op.cit., pp. 51-59. John Dawson of Liverpool to Boulton and Watt, 9th November 1790. Birmingham City Archives. Boulton and Watt/ Box4/3/12. Boulton and Watt to Beguye & Co of Nantes, 31st October 1791. BCA. Boulton and Watt, vol 15, p.19.

36 Galton, Samuel, junior, *To the Friends of the Monthly Meeting at Birmingham,* 1795. Galton Papers. BCA; Loggie, Val, McArdle, Jane and McLean, Rita, *op.cit.*; Smith, Barbara M.D., *op.cit.* (for the quotation see p. 147).

37 See Malcolm Dick, "Joseph Priestley and America" in this publication. His *Memoirs,* which were completed by his son for the years after 1794 note that Priestley "never interfered publicly in politics". An anti-slavery stance would be a political act in America at this time. *Memoirs of Dr Joseph Priestley, Written by himself (to the year 1795.) with a continuation to the time of his decease by his son, Joseph Priestley* (London, H.R. Allenson, 1904, reprint of 1809 edition), p. 109.

38 Bishop, David, "Some common bond": aspects of Birmingham's black international history" in Grosvenor, Mclean and Roberts, *op.cit.*, pp. 84-87. The records of the Female Society for the Relief of British Negro Slaves in Birmingham City Archives contain reports of activities and lists of members which enable the history of this pressure group to be traced.

Chapter 8

A SORRY END:
THE PRIESTLEY RIOTS OF 1791

Peter Leather

The "Priestley" Riots of July 1791 are one of the best-documented episodes in Birmingham history. The initial coverage of the riots in the local and national press led to a plethora of letters to the papers and "corrective" pamphlets. The victims were, after all, what Chris Upton has termed the "chattering classes" of their day [1]. Principal among these are at least three pamphlets all claiming to be "An Authentic Account" of the Riots [2]. But of course, prolific writer, William Hutton, a double victim of the Riots, had his say too [3], as did his daughter, Catherine, [4] and his friend William Russell's daughter [5]. Perhaps the final word should rightly go to Priestley himself [6].

The Riots are mentioned in all general histories of Birmingham, with detailed accounts in Dent [7], Gill [8] and Upton [9], and had a whole book dedicated to them by popular historian, Vivian Bird, at the time of the bicentenary in 1991 [10].

Joseph Priestley. Priestley Collection by Samuel Timmins, Birmingham City Archives.

More analytical accounts are given by Rose [11] and Martineau [12] (the latter addressing the single issue of whether the Riots were "managed") while the wider context is provided by Money [13].

With all that has been written, it might be imagined that everything possible is known about the Riots. However, the story remains incomplete, due to the

Richard Brinsley Sheridan.   Dr. Priestley.   Sir Cecil Wray.   Charles James Fox.   J. Horne Tooke.   Dr. Theophilus Lindsey.

"A Birmingham Toast, July 14th, 1791" by James Gillray. R.K. Dent, Old and New Birmingham: A History of the Town and its People (Birmingham, Houghton and Hammond, 1880).

preponderance of accounts by people favourable to Priestley, and limited research into "the other side" as told by local establishment figures and the London Press.

One of the few exceptions is the letter contesting Priestley's view of the Riots in one of the Authentic Accounts [14]. This accuses Priestley of inciting the violence against him while in no way excusing it [15]. After all, Priestley had famously written in January 1791, "I have long since drawn the sword and thrown away the scabbard, and am very easy about the consequences" [16]. However, to the modern mind, Priestley's defence – that his weapons had been words and with words only should they have been answered [17] – rings truer.

The circumstances leading up to the Riots are discussed in Rose [18]. The backdrop was years of growing tension between local dissenters and established churchmen connected with the campaign for the repeal of the Test and Corporation Acts; but the final spark was the political rift between radicals and conservatives brought about by the French Revolution of 1789.

Like others in Birmingham, Priestley was firmly on the side of both dissent and radicalism, although as always the lines were somewhat blurred – one of the leading radicals, James Keir, was in fact an Anglican.

One of the abiding national images of the Riots is a cartoon by leading caricaturist, James Gillray, showing Priestley and other well-known radicals, toasting "the King's head on a plate". It represents the "London" view of the Riots

The New Meeting, from The Riots at Birmingham, July 1791. Image by courtesy of James Rushton. The publication was republished by Arthur Bache Matthews, Birmingham in 1863.

which so much of the Birmingham literature is designed to counter. The cartoon refers to the event that set off the riots – a "Gallic Commemoration Dinner" in Birmingham on 14th July 1791 celebrating the second anniversary of the storming of the Bastille. It is of course a satire and not meant to be what actually happened – most of the people identified at the feast lived far from Birmingham and had nothing to do with Priestley except for some shared political views – but two "inaccuracies" are more significant from a local perspective. First, Priestley, shown as the proposer of the toast, did not actually attend the Dinner, as explained below; secondly, his pose, raising plate and chalice aloft, is more reminiscent of a Catholic communion than a Unitarian service, and brings to mind that on at least two occasions during the Riots, the mob is recorded as chanting "No Popery" – did they even know what they were rioting against?

Priestley had fully intended to go to the Dinner and had even done his best to get others to attend [19]. But things had heated up considerably following an announcement of the event published in *Aris's Birmingham Gazette*: "Any friend to freedom, disposed to join the intended temperate festivity, is desired to leave his name at the bar of the Hotel, where tickets may be had at five shillings each, including a bottle of wine" [20] [clearly an 18th Century use of the word "temperate"!]. This was accompanied by a statement that an attendance list would be published in a subsequent issue of the newspaper. The placing of this statement by the editor of the *Gazette* is seen by most Birmingham historians as a deliberate

The Rev Dr Priestley's House and Laboratory, Fair Hill, from The Riots at Birmingham, July 1791. Image by courtesy of James Rushton. The publication was republished by Arthur Bache Matthews, Birmingham in 1863.

attempt to scare people off and is interpreted by Martineau [21] as the first in a series of "conspiratorial" actions taken by the town's "establishment".

To make matters worse, a truly inflammatory handbill appeared in the streets at about the same time. It calls for "every Enemy to Civil and Religious Despotism" to "give his sanction to the Majestic Common Cause by a Public Celebration of the Anniversary". It goes on to compare the recently overturned system in France with that still running England [22]. The organisers of the Dinner were so determined to distance themselves from the handbill and its effect on the population that they published a second announcement in the Gazette on 13th July "to declare their entire disapprobation of all such Hand-bills, and their ignorance of the authors" and affirm their loyalty to "the Constitution". Despite this, there was still the threat of violence against the participants and a third announcement was prepared, cancelling the Dinner; but at this point the owner of the Hotel, possibly concerned at the loss of trade, proposed a compromise – the Dinner should go ahead but finish early, before any potential rioters had gathered [23].

At some stage during all this uncertainty, Priestley had decided not to attend, perhaps believing that, without him there, the Dinner could proceed in peace. He intended to spend a quiet evening in his home at Fair Hill, Sparkbrook.

Somewhere between 80 and 90 men attended the Dinner. They drank no fewer than 18 toasts [so that's why they needed a bottle of wine each!] including

Baskerville House, Residence of John Ryland Esq., from The Riots at Birmingham, July 1791. Image by courtesy of James Rushton. The publication was republished by Arthur Bache Matthews, Birmingham in 1863.

"The King and Constitution", "The Prince of Wales" and "Prosperity to the Town of Birmingham" as well as, more controversially, "The National Assembly and Patriots of France", "The New Constitution of France" and "The Rights of Man". They also toasted republican movements in the United States and Poland. Nevertheless, it was far short of the seditious declarations reported in the London press, in response to which the complete wording of the toasts was later published [24].

There had been some barracking of the diners as they entered the Hotel in Temple Row but it seemed that the hotelier's plan had worked when they departed peacefully. It was only after they had gone that a mob gathered outside the Hotel, accompanied by the town magistrates, Joseph Carles and Benjamin Spencer and the Under-Sheriff of Warwickshire, John Brooke. The fact that these three had been drinking with members of the mob and were now mingling with them outside the Hotel is used by Martineau [25] as further evidence that they were manipulating the situation to attack local radicals and particularly Priestley – however, it could also be argued that this is precisely what they should have been doing in order to try and take control of the situation (later in the Riots, William Hutton's son, Thomas, briefly won over the mob attacking his father's shop and got them to march with him at their head to the rescue of Bordesley Hall – although they quickly switched sides and joined the attackers when they got there) [26].

The House of William Russell, Esq., Showell Green, from The Riots at Birmingham, July 1791. Image by courtesy of James Rushton. The publication was republished by Arthur Bache Matthews, Birmingham in 1863.

The first act of violence was the stoning of the empty hotel but the mob soon moved on to more "worthy" targets in the shape of Priestley's New Meeting House on Moor Street and the nearby Old Meeting House in Worcester Street. It seems that Brooke may have bribed the mob to move on; if so this could have been simple self-interest as he owned a house near the hotel. Martineau contends that he went further, specifically recommending that they attack the Meeting Houses, and that he did this as part of a concerted plan with Carles and Spencer.

According to Martineau, the magistrate's first plan for the riots ended there, and they were as shocked as anyone to hear that the mob had moved on from the Meeting Houses and marched down the Stratford Road to destroy Priestley's house, library and laboratory at Fair Hill ("the most truly valuable and useful apparatus of philosophical instruments that perhaps any individual in this or any other country, was ever possessed of") [27]. It was at this point, he claims, that, seeking to control a riot that was threatening to get out of hand and make the most of it, they drew up a "hit-list" of houses the mob could target.

Certain aspects of what happened during the Riots do indeed suggest a degree of reason behind the madness. Several owners of properties were warned in advance of their fate and, in the most remarkable episode, the elderly lady tenanting a "targeted" house owned by John Taylor, was helped to move all her belongings to a safe distance before destruction commenced.

On the other hand, elements of the mob were clearly motivated by more basic desires than protecting the establishment, with Priestley's cellar given higher priority than his laboratory in the attack, and many looters joining in the fun. The same thing happened at Baskerville House on Easy Hill with tragic consequences for drunken rioters who were trapped in the building when it was set alight.

Priestley had fled Fair Hill when first news of the riots reached him and taken refuge in the Russell family's, as yet, safe house at Showell Green. One wonders once again to what extent Priestley may have been prepared for this contingency.

According to Miss Russell's account [28], the sounds of the mob's destruction of Fair Hill could be clearly heard by the terrified Russell and Priestley families, who had moved from the Showell Green house, now considered to be also under threat, to that of Mr Hawkes: "What were the emotions of our mind at this moment no one can imagine, unless they had beheld our countenances and heard the broken, short sentences that formed all the conversation that passed between us: yet the extreme agitation of our minds did not prevent us from admiring the divine appearance of the excellent Dr. Priestley".

In the early hours of the morning, the Russells and Priestleys returned to Showell Green, where the house had seemingly been spared (it was to be destroyed on the Saturday evening). No sooner had Priestley and his wife gone to bed than word came that the rioters were stirring again from their drunken slumbers on the lawns of Fair Hill and were heading this way intent on getting their hands on Priestley. The dazed Doctor and Mrs Priestley had to get dressed again and set off in a chaise through the back-lanes south of Birmingham to the safety of a friend's house near Dudley [29].

So it was that one of the greatest men ever to have lived in Birmingham made his ignominious exit, never to return. A few days later he was in London, writing his famous letter to the inhabitants of Birmingham, which appeared in Aris's Gazette on 25th July 1791. It ends: "At all events, we return you blessings for curses; and pray that you may soon return to that industry, and those sober manners, for which the inhabitants of Birmingham were formerly distinguished" [30].

Notes

1 Upton, Chris, *A History of Birmingham* (Phillimore, Chichester, 1993), p. 55.

2 A) *An Authentic Account of the Late Riots in the Town of Birmingham and its Vicinity, from the Commencement of Thursday, the 14th of July 1791, to the final Suppression on the 19th of the same month. Together with the Letter of Dr. Priestley, and an Answer thereto. Also, the several Letters of Wm. Russell and James Keir, Esqrs. With an Account of the Toasts drank at the Gallic Commemorative Meeting, at the Hotel, and a Literal Copy of the Seditious Hand-Bill, which is supposed to have given rise to these Riotous Proceedings* (Birmingham 1791);

B) *An Authentic Account of the Dreadful Riots in Birmingham, occasioned by the Celebration of the French Revolution, on the 14th of July, 1791, when the Property of the Inhabitants was destroyed to the amount of Four Hundred Thousand Pounds* (H.D. Symonds, London, 1791);

C) *An Authentic Account of the Riots in Birmingham, on the 14th, 15th, 16th, and 17th days of July, 1791. Also, the Judge's Charge, the Pleadings of the Counsel, and the Substance of the Evidence given on the Trials of the Rioters. And an Impartial Collection of Letters, &c.... The whole compiled, in order to preserve to posterity the Genuine Particulars ... of an Event, which attracted the Attention of Europe.* (Compiled by James Belcher, Birmingham, 1791 – Appendix 1792).

3   *A Narrative of the Riots in Birmingham, July 14th, 1791, particularly as they affected the Author*, in *The Life of William Hutton* (first published 1816, latest edition with introduction by Carl Chinn, Brewin, Studley, 1998) – Hutton says that he intended to publish this section separately "but my family would not suffer it to see the light" (p. 73).

4   *A Narrative of the Riots in Birmingham, July, 1791* ("Printed for private circulation among the descendents of those who suffered in those troublous times", Birmingham, 1875) – note the long delay before publication, long after Catherine and all others involved were dead.

5   Extensively quoted (along with Catherine Hutton) in Dent, Robert K, *Old and New Birmingham* (Birmingham, 1879), pp. 228-256.

6   Priestley, Joseph, *An Appeal to the Public, on the Subject of the Riots in Birmingham. To which are added, Strictures on a Pamphlet, intitled 'Thoughts on the Late Riot at Birmingham.'* (J. Thompson, Birmingham, 1792).

7   Dent, *op cit.*

8   Gill, Conrad, *History of Birmingham, Volume 1: Manor and Borough to 1865* (Oxford University Press, London, 1952).

9   Upton, *op cit.*

10 *The Priestley Riots, 1791, and the Lunar Society* (Birmingham and Midland Institute, Birmingham, 1991).

11 Rose, RB, "The Priestley Riots of 1791", *Past & Present*, Number 18 (November 1960) pp. 68-88 – also summarised in "Political History to 1832", Stephens, WB (ed), *A History of the County of Warwick, Volume VII: The City of Birmingham* (The Victoria History of the Counties of England, Oxford University Press, London, 1964) pp. 279-281.

12 Martineau, Denis, "Playing Detective: the Priestley Riots of 1791", *Birmingham Historian* Number 12, pp. 15-18 + Number 13, pp. 11-16.

13 Money, John, *Experience and Identity: Birmingham and the West Midlands 1760-1800* (Manchester University Press, Manchester, 1977).

14 (A) as cited above.

15 *ibid*, pp. 16-19.

16 *The Theological and Miscellaneous Works of Joseph Priestley* (edited by JT Rutt, Hackney, 1817-31) Volume 2, p. 9.

17 *An Authentic Account... (A), op cit*, pp. 13-16.

18 *op cit*, pp.68-72.

19 His invitation to William Hutton and its refusal are recorded by Catherine Hutton, *op cit*, quoted in Dent, *op cit*, p. 225.

20 Quoted in Upton, *op cit*, p. 53.

21 *op cit*, Part 2, p. 12.

22 Reproduced in *An Authentic Account ... (A), op cit*, p. 2f.

23 *ibid* ("Mr Russell's Refutation of a fallacious Account of the Toasts &c given in a London Print, called The Times, at the late Gallic Commemoration Dinner at the Hotel, Birmingham; addressed to the Editor of the Star, a London Paper"), p.20f.

24 *ibid*, p. 22ff.

25 *op cit*, Part 2, p. 12f.

26 Catherine Hutton, *op cit*, quoted in Dent, *op cit*, p. 237.

27 *An Authentic Account ... (A), op cit* ("Dr Priestley's Letter to the Inhabitants of the Town of Birmingham"), p. 14.

28 Dent, *op cit*, pp. 229-30.

29 *ibid*, p. 238.

30 *ibid*, pp. 248-9.

The most up-to-date published list of sources for the Priestley Riots is provided by Field, Clive D, "The Protestant Churches" in Chinn, Carl (ed), *Birmingham: Bibliography of a City* (University of Birmingham Press, Birmingham, 2003) pp. 99-101.

Chapter 9

FRIENDS REUNITED:
DR PRIESTLEY AND THE RUSSELLS
OF BIRMINGHAM

Shena Mason

When Joseph Priestley left Lord Shelburne's service in 1780 after some years as librarian and tutor, he went initially to London and spent time with scientific friends including Benjamin Franklin, but then at the suggestion of his brother-in-law, John Wilkinson, he decided to move to Birmingham. Dr and Mrs Priestley quickly made themselves at home in Birmingham and found congenial company. Through contacts with people already known to them, including Franklin, Josiah Wedgwood and the Wilkinsons, they would have had introductions to many of the leading townsfolk, especially the local scientific fraternity embodied in the Lunar Society. Priestley wrote later, "I consider my settlement in Birmingham as the happiest event of my life, being highly favourable to every object I had in view, philosophical or theological" [1].

Portrait of Joseph Priestley 1794. Priestley Collection by Joseph Timmins, Birmingham City Archives.

Among the earliest friends the Priestleys made in Birmingham were the Russells. William Russell (1740-1818) was the son of an ironmaster and had been educated for the commercial life. By 1770 he was exporting goods to Russia, Spain and America. He was to some extent a public figure, having served as Low Bailiff of Birmingham in 1768. In 1785 he was a member of the Birmingham Commercial Committee, and in 1787 was appointed a Warden of the Assay Office. He was moreover a leading Nonconformist. He helped Priestley to get established in Birmingham, providing him with the use of his own carriage and horses, and being largely instrumental in Priestley's appointment as minister to the New Meeting Unitarian chapel. William Russell lived with his wife, Martha, and his children, Martha, Mary and Thomas at Showell Green, near Moseley.

WILLIAM RUSSELL (1740-1818)
from a water colour.

Nonconformists, or "dissenters" made up much of Birmingham's commercial community; in many cases they were benefactors to the town, and were broadly tolerated. The French Revolution of 1789 changed that. It caused shock-waves which crossed the Channel and caused much political nervousness. Thereafter, any groups perceived as radical attracted suspicion. The fact that the dissenters saw the Revolution in France as an act of liberation of the masses

William Russell (1740-1818). A photo of the original painting hangs in the Assay Office in Birmingham, of which he was a Guardian and Warden 1787-1791 in Jeyes, S.H., The Russells of Birmingham (1911).

only served to deepen the mistrust with which they were viewed. These smouldering embers of resentment turned into a full-blown conflagration on the night of 14th July 1791.

On that evening, a dinner was planned at Dadley's Hotel in Temple Row, to mark the second anniversary of the storming of the Bastille and to commemorate the liberation of the French people. Inflammatory reports of the proposed celebration spread round the town beforehand, so much so that the diners themselves resolved to cancel or postpone it, but the hotel proprietor (no doubt thinking of his profit) assured them that such extreme action was unnecessary. The dinner duly took place, attended by, among others, William Russell – but not by Dr Priestley, for whom celebration dinners held no great appeal. Nevertheless, the gentlemen arriving for the dinner found themselves hissed and booed by a hostile crowd on the lookout for Dr Priestley. At about 8 p.m. the crowd began smashing the hotel windows [2]. Frustrated by Priestley's absence, the mob, chanting "*Church and King for ever!*" then moved on in search of their quarry. First they attacked Priestley's chapel, the New Meeting, and next his home. Mob hysteria, fuelled by

Destruction of Dr Priestley's House and laboratory, Fair Hill, Birmingham July 14th, 1791. After a picture sketched on the spot, now in the possession of Madame Belloc, London in Jeyes, S.H., The Russells of Birmingham (1911).

plundered alcohol, took over, and the homes of those who had been present at the dinner, and several others who had not, became additional targets.

In five days of mayhem, the houses of a number of prominent citizens were ransacked and burned. Some of the rioters died when they were too drunk to escape the flames which they themselves had started at John Ryland's home, on the site of the present Baskerville House.

Among those forced to escape were Priestley's friends, the Russell family. William Russell (51) was now a widower, Mrs Martha Russell having died in a coach accident the previous year; their daughters Martha (25) and Mary (23), and son Tom (16) were all still at home at Showell Green, which was one of the houses destroyed. The young Russells kept diaries which are still in Birmingham City Archives. Most of what follows is taken from their vivid accounts of the events of those five days and their subsequent travels.

After the dinner on that fateful evening of 14th July, William Russell returned home and was drinking tea with his family when news reached them that a rampaging mob was heading for Dr Priestley's house, Fair Hill at Sparkbrook. This news was followed shortly by the arrival in a chaise of the Priestleys themselves; in

The House of William Russell, Esq., Showell Green, from The Riots at Birmingham, July 1791. Image by courtesy of James Rushton. The publication was republished by Arthur Bache Matthews, Birmingham in 1863.

fear for their lives, they had escaped from their home and left it to its fate. Along with his house, Priestley lost all his scientific equipment and papers. While William Russell bravely saddled his horse and set out to try and reason with the mob, the Russell girls hastily packed some possessions. When their father returned, having been pelted with stones, it was decided that the Priestleys should be got out of harm's way and they were sent overnight to their married daughter's near Dudley. William Russell went off to renew his fruitless search for magistrates willing to do something to quell what was now a full-blown riot. Meanwhile, Mary, Martha and Tom Russell escaped on foot across the dark fields to Warstock, to the home of an old family servant where they spent the night [3].

Next day came the news that their home at Showell Green was in flames. The girls and their young brother set off that night to walk by moonlight to Alcester, nearly twenty miles away, hiding under hedges when mobs of rioters on horseback galloped by. At Alcester they were relieved to be rejoined by their father, who had brought their own chaise in which they travelled on to Stratford and thence to London. There they found the Priestleys, who had made their way south from Dudley. After a few days' rest the Russells returned to Birmingham, and stayed with an uncle in New Hall Street. Priestley did not dare to return; he spent the next few years in London. In 1793 his sons, Joseph, William and Henry emigrated to America, and in April 1794 Dr and Mrs Priestley followed them.

Priestley had promised William Russell that Mary and Martha should have a safe home with him in America if they ever wished to join him. That July the Russell family set out for the port of Falmouth, stopping at several places en route including Jamaica Inn on Bodmin Moor, which Mary Russell described in her diary as "The most miserable dirty place I ever saw to be called an Inn – they had fortunately a bit of Pork in the house which after waiting 2 hours for we got in steaks for our dinner with some very bad bread & potatoes. They had neither cheese nor butter & nothing but water to drink" [4].

Jamaica Inn held the dubious distinction of being the dirtiest inn Mary had ever seen only until she reached Falmouth, when she found herself in a yet dirtier one. The family spent a week in Falmouth waiting for their ship, and eventually set sail on 13th August 1794. Trouble struck just four days into the voyage, while they were still in the Channel, when their ship was intercepted by a French frigate and they were taken prisoner. Ordered to gather a few belongings and get into a small boat, the Russells grabbed some clothes and, prudently, their medicine chest. When the open boat drew alongside the frigate they found to their horror that they must climb up its cliff-like sides on a ladder. Martha, her gown soaked by a wave which had washed over the side of the small boat, was first up and wrote later "I shall never forget my feelings on finding myself at the top, 300 dirty, filthy, ragged looking sailors crowded on the deck to see us" [5].

New York City in 1768 in Jeyes, S.H., The Russells of Birmingham (1911).

For the next forty days, while the French ship hunted along the coastline for other prizes, they slept fully-dressed on the floor among the ship's stores and vermin, sharing one spoon for their food, the passing days marked by thrice-daily singing of the *Marseillaise*. Far from fainting with fear and disgust, Martha seems to have got a taste for life on board, writing of the exhilaration of chasing after other vessels at twelve knots, and waiting eagerly to see if the boarding party had found any potatoes in the captured ship – potatoes being something they were missing, evidently. They were also impressed with the French sailors' dancing: "the astonishingly light manner in which they move (many in wooden shoes) was a matter of surprise to us all, they appear to be particularly made to excel in dancing, for really I never saw any dancing master in England acquit himself better than these dirty, mean, awkward looking fellows"[6]. Mary Russell wrote that the French officers were keen to improve their English and asked the prisoners to hear them read and correct their pronunciation, offering to do the same in return in French "which we thought it right to consent to, tho' our minds were too unsettled to receive any benefit from their tuition"[7].That their minds were 'unsettled' is hardly to be wondered at, when Mary tells us that they had 'one teacup of water to wash in' and

> *we found we had no conveniency [WC] at all & were obliged to empty a tin we had with gingerbread in & use that – which we were very thankful we had, or I know not what we should have done as the only place there was opend into the Cabin where we always eat & where the officers some or other of them always were & some slept there – we were now obliged to get over many scruples of delicacy which at any other time we shou'd have thought impossible to have been done – I cannot describe how much we relished the gingerbread....*[8]

On 2nd September they were transferred to another ship off the French coast, and shortly after that to yet another, where at least the accommodation was better, but the food left much to be desired: four pounds of beef for thirty people, 'boiled to rags' and soup which they were "obliged to swallow without looking as there were all kinds of messes in it"[9]. These French ships were manned by crews whom Martha describes as smelling shockingly of garlic and swarming with "live creatures". At last, on 26th December 1794, after five months at sea, they were set ashore at the French port of Brest. There they bought themselves a carriage (the one in which they had travelled from Birmingham having been thrown overboard by their first captors) and set off for Paris, a journey of eighteen days.

The sisters' diaries describe life in Paris over the next six months. They first took lodgings in the Hôtel de Carouzel, opposite the Louvre, a suite of rooms with blue silk damask hangings, chairs, sofas, cut-glass chandeliers and inlaid oak floors. None of this luxury could compensate for the penetrating cold. One of their fellow residents was "Mrs Imlay" (Mary Wollstonecraft, then living in France with her American lover, Gilbert Imlay, as his wife). After a month the Russells moved to a pleasanter apartment overlooking the Tuilleries, but still it was so cold that the water froze as they stood by the fire washing their hands, and bread was scarce. In post-Robespierre Paris it was unwise to appear on the streets looking too clean or well-dressed. Sitting in on debates in the National Convention, they were unimpressed with the new French regime, Martha describing them as for the most part "dirty, mean, shabby-looking fellows... some in fur caps, others in red and blue caps, some apparently in dirty nightgowns, others shabby great coats, many that had not been shaved for a week at least, and some that had not a comb in their hair that day." The President had broken three bells trying to get silence [10].

To keep occupied and warm, the Russells spent much time in the Public Library. As Spring approached, they went to see the Cabinet of Natural History arranged by Buffon, and the Botanical Gardens. Mary wrote of Buffon's collection: 'The Cabinet is a very curious & valuable one tho the arrangement is by no means so pleasing or convenient as the British Museum' [11]. And of course they went shopping – At the Palais Royal, 'the beauty and elegance of the shops was beyond description at night when they were all lighted up, it was past conception enchanting' [12]. The women visited galleries, museums, cathedrals, abbeys, and the Sèvres china factory. At the Observatory, the guide told them a sixty-foot diameter telescope was on order ('Hershalls is only 44', wrote Martha). The guide showed them

> *several fine maps of the Moon & invited us to come some fine evening & see Saturn, & the Moon thro a telescope, they had three of Dollonds that magnified 3000 times – we accepted the good man's invitation & went a few evenings after to see Saturn, it was the most beautiful object vivid to a degree.... when we saw it three of the moons were visible.... The Moon also exhibited a far more beautiful appearance than I had ever before seen her – we thought we could plainly discover rocks & water & looked earnestly to discern the people...* [13]

Next time they visited the Observatory they found their guide had been arrested as a Jacobin and thrown into jail.

They enjoyed the theatre and Mary Russell sagely compared the English and French stage versions of heaven and hell, observing that at the Paris Opera 'the French heaven was I must confess much superior in taste and beauty to the English tho' the English hell was far more terrific and dreadfull than the French' [14]. The French off-stage 'hell' was dreadful enough: 'Madame Guillotine' had not retired

– William Russell and his son went to an execution where, wrote Mary, they saw sixteen people guillotined in thirteen minutes [15].

On some of their excursions and theatre visits they were accompanied by "Mrs. Imlay". Mary Wollstonecraft's *Thoughts on the Education of Daughters* had been published in 1787, and her best-known work *Vindication of the Rights of Woman* in 1792. Mary Russell found her conversation compelling: "she seemed to have much information & to be fond of communicating it… we went into her lodgings & found she had one fine little girl of eight months old & which she brought up quite on her own plan" [16].

On 20th June 1795 the Russells at last resumed their journey to America. They left Paris for Le Havre, from where they set sail for New York on the *Nancy* on 3 July. Among their fellow passengers was a "Mr Astor of New York". The voyage seems to have been a great contrast to their experiences in the Channel, with good quarters, good food and mainly good weather. Tom Russell kept a solemn log in which he recorded, five or six times a day, the weather conditions, compass bearing, sail carried and other vessels sighted. Rarely does he tell us anything else, but on 11th July at 10pm he noted "I saw a whale" [17]. As usual, Martha took a lively interest in events on board, one night recording in her journal:

> *This even'g the Capt catched a Shark, one of our steerage passengers had put a nice piece of fat ham in a net, & tyed it to drag it in the sea in order to soak out the salt a little, near this the Capt. had suspended a hook for the purpose of catching fish, towards evening the ham was gone & about an hour afterwards the shark was caught – the French man who had lost the ham immediately said he supposed his ham was in the belly, & if so, he hoped the Capt wd give it him – this diverted us very much – however the poor shark was dragged upon deck & his tail cut off, after this his head, & then his stomach opened, in which sure enough was the French man's ham, net and all together, which amidst a burst of laughter Capt. Butler rendered to the owner.* [18]

They dropped anchor in Sandy Hook on 21st August, and from that point Tom abandons his terse meteorological reports and launches into narrative. On 22nd August a pilot took them ashore, with Mr Astor, for the "extravagant" price of twenty dollars,

> *but however in compensation we had a charming sail of about 8 miles; as you approach the narrows the shore of Long Island on one side & Staten Island on the other, both high land, have a beautiful appearance, the Dutch built houses & Barns & some fields of Indian corn forming a pleasing & to us a*

new variety; after passing the narrows the prospect opens with a view of the Jersey shore & Long Island, on each side, several small isles interspersed & the spires of New York just visible through the mist. Having sailed by Governors Island on which is an insignificant fort, the town appears in full view with an air of nobleness & beauty...

The streets are in general narrow & ill disposed. The houses are very irregular in size & shape & a strange jumble of Brick Stone & Wood – the only good street is the Broad Way which is a noble one....[19]

Mary and Martha Russell's diaries both record their delight at the rural beauties of Staten Island after so long at sea. They stayed only a short time in New York, where yellow fever was rife, before setting off (in the coach they had bought months before at Brest) for Philadelphia, where they planned a reunion with their old friend Dr. Priestley. We can picture them, peering eagerly from the coach windows as, in Tom's words: "This being the first journey through the country was an interesting one. Our curiosity being all alive to discover something novel, left nothing that differed from Old England unobserved." Along the way, Mary noted 'wild flowers growing which are cultivated in English gardens with great care', great numbers of fir trees, and strange birds. She was impressed with the white-painted wooden houses in Newark, each with its neat garden. The route took them through Princetown, Elizabeth Town, Woodbridge, and Brunswick.

No sooner had they found lodgings in Philadelphia than Dr Priestley's son Joseph called on them and showed them round the town. "The streets are in general very broad and strait, the houses chiefly of brick & very neat, many of them very large & spacious. We went into the Senate House & Congress Hall which are both very neat. The State House is a very good building & the publick gardens belonging to it very agreeable, planted by Mr Samuel Vaughan of London," wrote Mary. It was, however, very hot, and very dear – a week's board and lodging cost them ten dollars [20].

After showing them the sights of Philadelphia, young Joseph Priestley accompanied the travellers to his parents' home at Northumberland, seven days' coach-ride away. "Dr P-s family all well & very glad to see us, the situation of North d is beautifull just on the forks of the Susquehanna it is a small place & the roads about it are very good," wrote Mary approvingly [21]. Her brother described how settlers would clear a piece of ground and build first of all a "bark house". Later the neighbours would all help to raise a "log house" in a day, followed by an evening of celebration. Later still, when a sawmill was established, they would build a "frame house" and use the old log house as a barn or stable. Often, having reached this point, the settlers would move on to some fresh area to begin the process over again, and the frame houses would be bought by incomers. Dr Priestley had bought such a frame house, "and it is fitted up with all that neatness for which his wife is well known, but still it is a mere hut in comparison with the one they lived in formerly. His eldest son, Joseph, lives with his wife in a large brick house. William and Henry, his other sons, cultivate a farm three miles from town. The Doctor is enveloped in his studies..."[22]

Although Mary thought Northumberland "beautiful", Tom was not convinced, writing that though some might think it an ideal place for Priestley to settle in,

> *an impartial person would be far from making the same conclusion. There is not a family except his own & perhaps Mr Cooper [of Manchester] with whom Dr P can enjoy the kind of society to which he has been always accustomed. From its remote situation, there is very little communication with Philad[a]..... In addition to these inconveniences, the town & neighbourhood is far from being healthy: in the autumn they are commonly afflicted with the fever & ague; it is very general, this fall several of the Drs family have had it, but none have been so much afflicted with it as Henry, who is very much debilitated by successive fits.* [23]

Tom could not understand how people could give up a comfortable life in town for such voluntary exile. The Russells had to decide where to make their home, but it was not easy: "As Dr Priestley was settled there, it would undoubtedly have been an additional inducement to us to have fixed in the same place, could we have reconciled ourselves to other circumstances, but the sacrifice would have been greater than we could have justified to ourselves, & we consequently abandoned the idea"[24].

The Russells stayed for about two weeks with the Priestleys, returning to Philadelphia at the end of September. There they decided to take a house for a year and give themselves time to get to know the country before choosing where to make their long-term home. But first they went back to Boston to collect some of their furniture from storage. En route they passed through Newhaven, "one of the first settled places in this eastern part & .... chief witness of those horrid scenes of monstrous tyranny & barbarous enthusiasm which the first inhabitants, who had themselves but just escaped from persecution, exercised in the name of religion: for their government was then ecclesiastical, to the great misfortune not only of their own brethren but of the poor Indians, thousands of whom were massacred under the banners of the Lamb..."[25]

Another town on their route to and from Boston was Middletown, Connecticut, which seems to have made an immediate and favourable impression; Tom says they were all, *truly enchanted with the richness, fertility, beauty & variety of the country on every side, & as far as the attractions of Nature are likely to influence our settlement we shall probably meet with no other situation where they are so powerful, & if they are so strong now what must they be when arrayed in all the blooming charms of Spring. Now that we have left behind us all those attractions which result from the society of those we love or esteem, these charms seem to be the most powerful of any, especially where a healthy climate procures the enjoyment of them.* [26]

Back in Philadelphia for the winter, the Russells had a visit from Dr and Mrs Priestley. The Priestleys arrived in January 1796, the Doctor bearing a set of sermons he had written on the subject of *Evidences of Revelation*. Preaching these in a local church at the rate of one a day, the visit lasted until April. Tom comments that when you have someone living under your roof they often turn out to be rather different from what you expected and gives us this insight into Priestley's character:

Dr Priestley is undoubtedly a very virtuous, learned & agreeable man & his name will be handed down to posterity as a great philosopher & as one who dared to reduce religion to the laws of reason & common sense... but yet he is not one with whom one could enjoy the pleasure of domestic intercourse. In the little occurrences of a family he is apt to be discontented & fretful. In case every thing does not go on to his mind he will be upon the figits [sic] until it is rectified

City of Middletown, Connecticut in 1825 in Jeyes, S.H., The Russells of Birmingham (1911).

& perhaps for some time after. In short he displays a degree of selfishness which I should never have suspected from one who acts so disinterestedly in greater things; but there are few men who can lay a just claim to the title of a consistent character through all events & circumstances. He was very much disgusted at the depravity of manners, at the narrow worldly minded tempers of the Philadelphians, among whom he found very few with whom he could enjoy that enlightened conversation he had been used to in England & for which his attainments in science have excited so great a relish. [27]

Tom adds that Dr Priestley returned to Northumberland without regret, a feeling which was perhaps shared by his hosts! Later in the year Priestley was to lose first his son, Henry, and then his wife, a loss he felt deeply. William and Tom Russell travelled back to Northumberland to visit him at least once, but William's deafness was becoming so profound as to make it impossible for him to enjoy his old friend's conversation, and the visits stopped.

By the autumn of 1796 the Russells' thoughts turned back to Middletown, Connecticut. William and his son returned there and took an eight-year lease on a house, described as a large brick building with fine views all round, four rooms to each floor, with four acres of land. William Russell also took thirty acres of farmland just outside the town. Then they went back to Philadelphia to collect Martha and Mary. The family soon settled in at Middletown and wasted no time getting to know the local people, whom they seem to have found friendly and welcoming. The climate was kinder than in Philadelphia. Winter, though cold, had...

...some advantages which England cannot boast, the useful as well as pleasant custom of sleighing much contributes to enliven the Country at that dreary season.... Every one then seems to be open to the pleasures of friends & society & the frequent chearful ringing of bells which are fixed to the horses of every sleigh seem quite in unison with the general gaiety around – we were all much pleased with the exercise of sleighing for tho' it must be very cold to be good sleighing, yet if well secured by warm clothing the sensation one feels when gliding so rapidly along is very pleasant. The first time we rode in a sleigh the whole Country had the most beautiful appearance imaginable – There had been the night before a rain which had frozen as fast as it had fallen & by that means encrusted every blade of grass which the snow had not covered as well as every shrub & tree with clear transparent ice 5 or 6 times as thick as itself. The orchards had a most beautiful effect as their icy burdens bent their boughs in a very graceful manner & made them assume many fantastic forms & which the rays of the sun rendered frequently too dazzling to look at. All the rails of the fences were fringed with this brilliant crystal & the whole face of the Country had a kind of magic appearance [28].

Though clearly entranced with the landscape, the Russells were unhappy at finding slavery prevalent; "the cruel manner in which they were in general treated must shock the feelings of every friend to humanity whose heart is not hardened by education & habit of regarding the Negroes in a light not superior to Beasts", wrote Mary. She was struck by the imagination of one young slave girl who, on seeing ice for the first time, was asked what she thought it was, "to which she replied she thought it looked like water asleep, a very expressive and ingenious idea" [29].

As winter gave way to spring, work began in the garden. They sowed flower and vegetable seeds, and built a bower to give them some shade in the summer where they might drink tea with friends. The land and the river gave forth food in abundance: "We have not now the least want of a Market… we have in our larder very fine veal, mutton, fowls, salmon & shad & plenty of poultry in our yard & salt meat in our cellar. We have not yet eat asparagus but shall in a day or two…" [30]

Life went on comfortably in Middletown, until in 1798 came the beginning of the end of the Russells' American sojourn. One of William Russell's friends in England, James Skey, who had already been widowed twice, went out to Middletown to marry Martha Russell. Skey sailed from Liverpool to Cork and then embarked on the *Chesapeake* bound for Philadelphia on 26th August. He, too, kept a journal of the voyage – recording on 7th October, "had boiled dolphin for dinner, very indifferent food, dry & resembling boiled veal". A flying fish trying to escape the dolphin had landed on deck, but the ship's cat had eaten it before Skey had chance to recover and preserve it as a specimen. Skey also noted the recipe for his favourite dish on board, "sea pye": "take thin slices of pork, which place at the Bottom of the saucepan, cut the meat of a Fowl or other flesh in small pieces, season it, slice onions & potatoes, add sweet Herbs, parsley &c & sprinkle a little flour to thicken your Soup – and as it stews, make your paste to cover the top – fill the Vessel with Water & let it all stew together" [31].

James Skey landed on 26th October and wasted no time getting away from Philadelphia. There was a tented city of some ten thousand people camped on the outskirts of the city hoping to escape the fever, which had already killed several thousand people in Philadelphia and New York. Having got safely away and arrived in Middletown, Skey was "affectionately welcomed by the best of Women" and had "the satisfaction to contemplate the inexpressible valuable acquisition of a virtuous, faithfull & affectionate Friend & Partner in domestic life and a kind and tender Parent to my Children" [32].

Skey's impressions of American life and manners are less complimentary than those of the Russells, possibly reflecting a different mindset and perhaps some disappointed expectation of deference to "the old country". He thought the morals, manners and discipline lax, and "the general conduct of the females… very forward & indiscreet." He described the people generally as small-minded and uninterested in anything but their own lives and their own country, and instanced their reception of Dr Priestley, who judging from a letter to Skey written on 7th November 1798 had not found the degree of freedom of thought in America which he had expected:

> *I find myself exposed to more gross abuse here on account of my supposed attachment to the cause of France than I was in England, tho' I have nothing to do, or say about the politics of the Country, which indeed I hardly give any attention to, looking as I continually do towards Europe as the great Theatre of interesting transactions* [33].

James Skey and Martha Russell were married in Middletown on 13th December 1798; the following May they left for England. Two years later Mary Russell and her brother also set out for home, followed shortly afterwards by their father.

It is clear from the diaries that though they relished the adventure and experience of being in America and enjoyed life in Middletown, the Russells missed the intellectual life of Birmingham and regular contact with English society. Yet Mary's account of the voyage home – in which she describes the high sails of the ship as "sky scrapers" – is tinged with sadness, for her father could not return to England with them because England was still at war with France, and he owned an estate near Caen, the purchase of which had been negotiated for him by his Birmingham agent, Zacheus Walker. As a French landowner it was not safe for him to return to his native country, so he settled in France, spending his time reading the works of Erasmus Darwin, creating a garden and missing his daughters and

JAMES SKEY (1754–1838)
From a miniature by J. MILLAR (1797)

James Skey (1754-1838), from a miniature painting by James Millar in Jeyes, S.H., The Russells of Birmingham (1911).

old friends like Dr Priestley, who died in America in 1804. William Russell became a French citizen in 1807. That year his daughter, the brave, intrepid Martha Skey died, and in 1810 James Skey married his fourth wife, her sister, Mary Russell. Skey campaigned for his father-in-law to be allowed to return to England, which was finally permitted in 1814. William Russell spent the last four years of his life with his daughter and son-in-law at Upton-on-Severn, and was buried at St Philip's, Birmingham, in 1818, twenty-seven years after his home at Showell Green was destroyed by the anti-Priestley mob.

Notes

1   *Memoirs of Dr Priestley*, centenary edition (1904).
2   Dent, R.K., *Old and New Birmingham* (1878).
3   Jeyes, S.H., *The Russells of Birmingham* (1911).
4   *Diary of Mary Russell*, Vol. I, Birmingham City Archives [BCA] ZZ324, 660357A.
5   *Diary of Martha Russell*, Vol. I, BCA ZZ324, 660349A.
6   *Ibid.*
7   *Diary of Mary Russell*, Vol. I, BCA ZZ324, 660357A.
8   *Ibid.*
9   *Ibid.*
10 *Diary of Martha Russell*, Vol. II, BCA MS ZZ324:660349B.
11 *Diary of Mary Russell*, Vol. II, BCA ZZ324, 660357B.
12 *Ibid.*
13 *Diary of Martha Russell*, Vol. II, BCA ZZ324, 660349B.
14 *Diary of Mary Russell*, Vol. IV, MS ZZ324:660357C, Birmingham City Archives.
15 *Diary of Mary Russell*, BCA ZZ324, 660357.
16 *Diary of Mary Russell*, Vol. I, BCA ZZ324, 660357A.
17 *Diary of Thomas Russell*, Vol.I, BCA ZZ324, 660352A.
18 *Diary of Martha Russell*, Vol. III, BCA ZZ324, 660349C.
19 *Diary of Thomas Russell*, Vol.I, BCA ZZ324, 660352A.
20 *Diary of Mary Russell*, Vol. III, MS ZZ324: 660357B, BCA.
21 *Ibid.*
22 *Diary of Thomas Russell*, Vol. I, BCA ZZ324, 660352A.
23 *Diary of Thomas Russell*, Vol. I, BCA ZZ324, 660352A.
24 *Ibid.*
25 *Ibid.*
26 *Ibid.*
27 *Ibid.*
28 *Diary of Mary Russell*, Vol. IV, BCA ZZ324, 660357C.
29 *Diary of Mary Russell*, Vol. IV, BCA ZZ324, 660357C.
30 *ibid.*
31 *Diary of James Skey*, BCA ZZ324, 660359.
32 *ibid.*
33 *ibid.*

Chapter 10

JOSEPH PRIESTLEY AND AMERICA

Malcolm Dick

Joseph Priestley spent the last ten years of his life from 1794 to 1804 in the United States of America, where he continued to write theology, investigate science and add to his reputation as a radical. He was never completely alone, but the death or departure of members of his family and his location in Northumberland, Pennsylvania meant that he developed his ideas away from the stimulus of an urban culture and distant from the friends who had sustained him in Birmingham [1].

On 8th April, 1794, at 61 years of age, he left the United Kingdom, never to return. His house at Fair Hill, just outside Birmingham, with its library and laboratory was destroyed in 1791 by a "Church and King" mob. Though Priestley moved to Hackney, London, he was shunned by many of his former

Chemical Philosophers of the Present Day, Dr Priestley. The apotheosis of Joseph Priestley. The scientist ascends into the heavens with the aid of an eagle. Priestley Collection by Samuel Timmins, Birmingham City Archives.

contacts and reviled in cartoons and the conservative press for his anti-establishment views and ideological sympathy with the ideas of the French Revolution. In 1793 Britain was at war with Revolutionary France and Priestley was not safe in England.

Priestley was accompanied by his wife, Mary and his three sons, Joseph, William and Henry. His daughter Sarah remained in England with her husband William Finch. Priestley was offered a post at the University of Pennsylvania in Philadelphia, but he turned this down. Instead, he moved to Northumberland, a small settlement of about one hundred houses which was a coach journey of seven days from Philadelphia. Priestley's sons hoped to establish a haven nearby for English nonconformists who faced discrimination and persecution at home. For a time, this looked like a possibility, but the scheme did not come to fruition [2].

When Priestley left Britain he was, in effect, a refugee. In 1797 he wrote a poignant publication which revealed empathy towards those who were in a similar position to himself. In the *Case for Poor Emigrants*, Priestley quoted from the Old Testament: "Thou shalt not oppress a stranger; for ye know the heart of a stranger" (Exodus 22, 9) and "Love ye, therefore, the stranger. For ye were strangers in the land of Egypt." (Deuteronomy 10, 19). In these verses, he claimed, Moses was calling on the Israelites, who had been refugees in a foreign land, to show compassion to newcomers. Priestley applied this idea to the people of the United States: "permit me, who am myself a stranger among you, to recommend to your favourable notice, and charitable assistance, the various strangers, or emigrants, from different parts of Europe, and the West Indies islands, who are now crowding the shores of America" [3]. Many of these, like himself were escaping from persecution, war or revolution in their homelands.

Joseph Priestley House, Northumberland, Pennsylvania, from the south-east showing Priestley's laboratory. Birmingham City Archives, Priestley Collection by Samuel Timmins.

In Northumberland, Priestley was able to settle and build a wooden-framed house with exterior clapboards. His activity, at least in part, began to resemble his life in England. He preached sermons, promoted education in the locality and acquired scientific apparatus for a laboratory and books for his library [4]. One of Priestley's companions in America was Thomas Cooper, whose family bleached cloth in Manchester. Cooper's knowledge - he later became Professor of Geology at the University of Pennsylvania - probably enabled him to help Priestley's scientific experimentation [5]. Priestley was a productive scientist and writer in Pennsylvania. He identified carbon monoxide, which he called "heavy inflammable air", as a distinctive gas and he published more than thirty scientific papers. He also wrote over a dozen religious works, including his *History of the Christian Church* in six volumes [6]. Priestley, nevertheless, was without the close intellectual companionship which had marked his time in Britain and his isolation may have affected the quality of the scientific work he pursued [7].

Priestley rejected invitations to live in the more cosmopolitan surroundings of Philadelphia and the quiet provincial town of Northumberland remained Priestley's home until his death. Nevertheless, he visited Philadelphia many times where he founded the local Unitarian Church and met George Washington, John Adams and Thomas Jefferson [8]. Jefferson was already known to members of the Lunar Society and had been educated by one of the Lunar men, William Small, at the College of William and Mary, in Williamsburg, Virginia [9]. Priestley recognised the potential of the United States as a centre for scientific discovery. During his final visit to Philadelphia he told the local Philosophical Society that: "having been obliged to leave a country which has been long distinguished by discoveries in science, I think myself happy by my reception in another which is following its example, and which already affords a prospect of its arriving at equal eminence" [10].

Priestley's reputation as an extreme radical affected his reception. In 1799, he wrote *Letters to the Inhabitants of Northumberland* which marked him out as a sympathiser with the French Revolution and led to his investigation under the Alien and Sedition Acts which had been passed during the administration of John Adams. When Thomas Jefferson became President in 1800, Priestley was back in favour and the former consulted him during the design of the curriculum for the University of Virginia [11].

The presence of slavery in the United States was something that must have confronted Priestley. His Birmingham anti-slavery sermon of 1788 had marked him as an opponent of both the slave trade and slavery itself, but it does seem as if the Priestley household had to compromise its principles and a black slave was hired by the week because it was impossible to find a full-time maid [12]. Priestley's companion, Thomas Cooper, refers to the fact that his wife was "very uncomfortable" because of the problems entailed in securing labour for their household [13].

Priestley's personal life was affected by the death and departure of most of his family. In 1795, Henry, his youngest son, died of a fever and his wife, Mary, died of tuberculosis on 17th September in the following year [14]. She had been particularly adept at managing Priestley's household since their marriage, which had allowed Priestley "to give my whole time to my pursuits, which was an unspeakable advantage to me" [15]. In 1800, another son, William left Northumberland for Louisiana with his wife, Margaret. Amongst his immediate family, only his son Joseph remained with him until the end [16].

On 3rd February 1804, Priestley started to conduct a scientific experiment, but he was unable to complete it due to ill health and he went to bed in his library. On 6th February he dictated some revisions to a manuscript he was writing to one of his sons, Joseph, and an assistant. When he was satisfied with the changes he announced: "That is right. I have now done." Shortly afterwards he died peacefully at the age of 71. His son, Joseph, daughter-in-law, Elizabeth, their children and his friend Thomas Cooper were present at his death. He was buried close to his home. Thomas Jefferson described Priestley as "one of the few lives precious to mankind" [17].

Joseph Priestley the younger lived in the family home until 1811, when he returned to England. In 1874, chemists from across the United States came to the house in Northumberland to commemorate the centenary of the identification of oxygen. The meeting led to the creation of the American Chemical Society in 1876. Several families inhabited the dwelling until 1919, when it was acquired on behalf of Pennsylvania State College. In 1955, it was offered to the Commonwealth of Pennsylvania and in 1970 Joseph Priestley House was opened as a Museum. Since then a programme of activities have led to the restoration of the building and laboratory and the acquisition of period furniture and books, scientific apparatus, clocks and personal items that have a Priestley provenance. In 1994, the American Chemical Society designated Priestley's house a National Historic Chemical Landmark [18].

Gravestone of Dr Priestley in the Cemetery of Northumberland, Pennsylvania. "To the memory of the Rev Dr Joseph Priestley who departed this life on the 6th February 1804, Anno Etatis LXXI. "Return unto thy rest O my soul for the Lord has dealt bountifully with thee. I will lay me down in peace & sleep till I awake in the morning of the resurrection." Birmingham City Archives, Priestley Collection by Samuel Timmins.

Joseph Priestley House provides the people of the United States with a memorial to one of the major figures of the Eighteenth-Century Enlightenment and a means of learning about his importance as a religious figure, scientific pioneer, educational innovator and radical political theorist and campaigner.

Notes

1   The main source for Priestley's time in America is *Memoirs of Dr Joseph Priestley, Written by himself (to the year 1795.) with a continuation to the time of his decease by his son, Joseph Priestley* (London, H.R. Allenson, 1904, reprint of 1809 edition).

2   M. Andrea Bashore, "Joseph Priestley and His American Home" in *The East Central Intelligencer*, The Newsletter of the East-Central American Society for

Eighteenth Century Studies, N.S., Vol. 16, No. 2, May 2002. See also Shena
Mason, "Friends Re-United: Dr Priestley and the Russells of Birmingham" above.

3   *Observations on the Increase of Infidelity* (Thomas Dobson, Philadelphia,
    1797). Second edition. I am grateful to Gron Tudor Jones for this reference.

4   Bashore, *op.cit.*

5   Cooper was a friend and correspondent of James Watt junior and his letters to
    his friend, which are held in Birmingham City Archives, provide an insight
    into Priestley's life in America.

6   Bashore, op.cit.

7   P. M. Jones, "The Life and Times of Dr Joseph Priestley" in this publication.
    An article which discusses the impact of Priestley's relative intellectual
    isolation in America upon his scientific work is Michael Conlin, "Joseph
    Priestley's American defence of phlogiston reconsidered", *Ambix*, 43 (1996).

8   Anon, *Scientist*, leaflet produced by Joseph Priestley House, Northumberland
    County, PA (Pennsylvania Historical and Museum Commission); Bashore, *op.cit.*

9   For an account of Jefferson's relationship with Small see Martin Richard
    Clagett, *William Small, 1734-1775, Teacher, Mentor, Scientist.*
    PhD Dissertation, Virginia Commonwealth University, April, 2003, pp.171-181.
    Jenny Uglow, *The Lunar Men: The Friends who made the Future 1730 – 1810*
    (London, Faber and Faber, 2002), p.82, 258, 493-4.

10 Curt Suplee, *Joseph Priestley: Discover of Oxygen*
    (Washington, American Chemical Society, 2001), p.6.

11 Bashore, *op.cit.*

12 Duncan Hirsch, Alison, "The Priestley House" in *Pennsylvania Trail of
    History Guide* (Mechanicsburg, Pennsylvania, Stackpole Books), p.33.
    I am grateful to Tricia Mason for supplying this reference.

13 Thomas Cooper to James Watt Junior, April 4 1796.
    Birmingham City Archives. MIV Bundle C Folder 13 of 16, nos 121-130.

14 Bashore, *op.cit.*

15 Joseph Priestley to his sister, Mrs Crouch in Leeds,
    England, from Northumberland, 3rd October 1796.
    Birmingham City Archives, Volume of Priestley Collection
    by Samuel Timmins, IIR10 73499.

16 Bashore, *op.cit.*

17 Bashore, *op.cit.*
    I am grateful to Kenneth Hudson for supplying me with copies of newspaper
    cuttings describing the circumstances of Priestley's death.

18 *Ibid.*; Suplee, *op.cit.*, p.7.

Chapter 11

THE PRIESTLEY COLLECTION IN BIRMINGHAM CENTRAL LIBRARY

Patrick Baird

Situated on the sixth floor of Birmingham Central Library and housed in an elaborate wooden and glass bookcase is a collection of books, pamphlets and news cuttings relating to the life and works of Dr Joseph Priestley. Collected over decades, the collection includes materials written by the great man himself and items about him compiled by others.

All aspects of his life are covered including his scientific research with titles such as: *Experiments on the generation of air from water; with experiments relating to the decomposition of dephlogisticated and inflammable air* (1793), his life as a non-conformist minister: *The Proper constitution of a Christian Church, considered in a sermon, at the New Meeting House in Birmingham, with discourse relating to the present state of Rational Dissenter* (1782), the Riots of 1791: *An Appeal to the public, on the subject of the riots in Birmingham* (1792) and his personal life: *Memoirs of Dr Joseph Priestley, to the year 1795,written by himself ,with a continuation by his son ,J Priestley; and observations on his writings by T Cooper and Rev W Christie and four posthumous discourses* (1806).

A

S E R M O N

ON THE SUBJECT OF

THE SLAVE TRADE;

DELIVERED TO A SOCIETY OF

PROTESTANT DISSENTERS,

AT THE

NEW MEETING, IN BIRMINGHAM;

AND PUBLISHED AT THEIR REQUEST.

By JOSEPH PRIESTLEY, LL. D. F.R.S.

—— And hath made of one blood all nations of men
to dwell on all the face of the earth.
ACTS xvii. 26.

BIRMINGHAM,
PRINTED FOR THE AUTHOR, BY PEARSON AND ROLLASON;
AND SOLD BY J. JOHNSON, NO. 72, ST. PAUL'S CHURCH-YARD, LONDON.
MDCCLXXXVIII.
[PRICE ONE SHILLING.]

Title page to Joseph Priestley, A Sermon on the Subject of the Slave Trade... (Birmingham, 1788). Priestley Collection, Birmingham Central Library.

Altogether the collection consists of approx. 400 volumes and one of the most interesting guides to it is *A Bibliography of Priestley* compiled by Ronald E Crook and published by the Library Association in 1966.

Chapter 12

JOSEPH PRIESTLEY:
A GUIDE TO FURTHER STUDY

Malcolm Dick

Priestley was a prolific writer. His publications were collected into 26 volumes in Rutt's early Nineteenth-Century edition of his works and the collection of Priestley's individual books, pamphlets, articles and sermons fill a large bookcase on Floor 6 of Birmingham Central Library. Priestley has also been the subject of several biographies, but none do complete justice to his personality, intellect and significance, probably because of the breadth of his interests and activities. Published material has largely focused on his role as a scientist, theologian or political theorist. A number of authors in this publication identify the secondary and primary sources available to the researcher. Several biographies do not escape from the "great man" theory of history. They fail to explore him critically or locate him adequately in the context of his times. There remain several opportunities for the writing of serious studies of Priestley for the general reader and academic. Priestley still awaits a biographer of the quality of Desmond King-Hele, whose biography of Erasmus Darwin, Priestley's Lunar Society colleague, is wide-ranging, scholarly and readable.

Manuscript items are scattered or in short supply, as Peter Jones indicates in his contribution to this publication. Priestley is not as well-served by surviving archival sources as his friends and contemporaries, Matthew Boulton, Erasmus Darwin, James Watt and Josiah Wedgwood. A search on A2A (www.a2a.org.uk), the English strand of the UK Archives Network, reveals several collections of materials, but in most of these there are very few helpful sources. Birmingham City Archives and the Special Collections Department of Information Services at the University of Birmingham hold several letters. The volume of items on Joseph Priestley, collected by Samuel Timmins in the Nineteenth-Century, held at Birmingham City Archives, is a valuable compilation of letters, printed materials and visual sources, including cartoons.

The destruction of Priestley's home at Fair Hill, near Birmingham, in 1791 not only destroyed manuscript sources, but also physical evidence of his life and

Examples of Joseph Priestley's Bookplates. Priestley Collection by Samuel Timmins, Birmingham City Archives.

scientific work as well. There are few surviving items in England with a demonstrable Priestley provenance. The collections of Birmingham Museums & Art Gallery contain a few objects which commemorate Priestley's achievements and a portrait of Mrs Mary Priestley, which is held at Soho House. The Museum created in Joseph Priestley House, Northumberland, Pennsylvania, USA is one way of gaining an insight into Priestley's experience and importance (see the essay, "Joseph Priestley and America" in this publication).

Websites provide a useful starting point for the individual who wants to find out about Priestley. A search for "Joseph Priestley" will lead to a lot of hits. In most cases, the information has little substance. One detailed biographical source is http://www.woodrow.org/teachers/chemistry/institutes/1992/Priestley.html (I am grateful to Roy Billingham for this reference). During 2005, relevant material will be uploaded to the Revolutionary Players website, www.revolutionaryplayers.org.uk, as a result of the "Joseph Priestley and Birmingham Project".

Select Booklist
Anderson, R.G.W. and Lawrence, Christopher (eds.),
Science, Medicine and Dissent: Joseph Priestley (1733-1804)
Papers celebrating the 250th anniversary of the birth of Joseph Priestley....
(London, Wellcome Trust/ Science Museum, 1987).

Autobiography of Joseph Priestley, with an introduction by Jack Lindsay
(Bath, Adams and Dart, 1970).

Clark, John Ruskin, *Joseph Priestley: a comet in the system*
(USA, Torch Publications, 1990).

Farrar, K.R., *Dr Joseph Priestley, his Life and Work*
(North Western Museum of Science & Industry, n.d.).

Fruchtman, J, Jr, *The Apocalyptic Politics of Richard Price and Joseph Priestley:
A Study in Late Eighteenth-Century English Republican Millennialism*
(Philadelphia, American Philosophical Society, 1983).

Gibbs, *Joseph Priestley: Adventurer in Science and Champion of Truth*
(London, Nelson, 1965).

Holt, Anne, *A Life of Joseph Priestley* (London, Oxford University Press, 1931).

King-Hele, Desmond, *Erasmus Darwin: A Life of Unequalled Achievement*
(London, Giles de la Mare, 1999).

Lodge, Oliver, "Joseph Priestley", in Muirhead, J. H.,
Nine Famous Birmingham Men (Birmingham, Cornish Brothers, 1909).

Orange, A. D., *Joseph Priestley* (Aylesbury, Shire Publications, 1974).
This short publication is suitable for children.

Passmore, J.A., *Priestley's Writings on Philosophy, Science and Politics*
(London, Collier Macmillan, 1965).

Porter, Roy, *Enlightenment* (London, Penguin, 2000).

Rutt, J.T. (ed.), *The Theological and Miscellaneous Works of Joseph Priestley*,
26 Vols. (London, Smallfield, 1817-32).

Rutt, J. T., *Life and Correspondence of Joseph Priestley*, 2 vols.
(London, 1831-32).

Schofield, Robert E, *The Enlightened Joseph Priestley: A Study of his Life and
Works from 1773 to 1804*
(Philadelphia, PA, Pennsylvania State University Press, 2004).

Schofield, Robert E, *The Enlightenment of Joseph Priestley: A Study of his Life
and Works from 1733 to 1773*
(Philadelphia, PA, Pennsylvania State University Press, 1997).

Schofield, Robert E, *The Lunar Society of Birmingham:A Social History of
Provincial Science and Industry in Eighteenth-Century England*
(Oxford, Clarendon Press, 1970).

Uglow, Jenny, *The Lunar Men: The Friends who made the Future 1730 – 1810*
(London, Faber and Faber, 2002).

Chapter 13

THE WORDS OF JOSEPH PRIESTLEY: SOME EXAMPLES

Malcolm Dick

Human Rights and Equality

Every man, when he comes to be sensible of his natural rights, and to feel his own importance, will consider himself as fully equal to any other person whatever.
An Essay on the First Principles of Government (1768).

The Greatest Happiness of the Greatest Number

It must necessarily be understood, therefore whether it be expressed or not, that all people live in society for their mutual advantage; so that the good and happiness of the members, that is the majority of the members of any state is the great standard by which everything relating to that state must finally be determined.
An Essay on the First Principles of Government (1768).

The Right to Power and Property

The whole system of right to power, property, and everything else in society, must be regulated by the same consideration; the decisive question, when any of these subjects are examined, being what is it that the good of the community requires?
An Essay on the First Principles of Government (1768).

On Liberty

If I be asked what I mean by *liberty*, I should choose, for the sake of greater clearness, to divide it into two kinds, *political* and *civil*; and the importance of having clear ideas on this subject will be my apology for innovation. POLITICAL LIBERTY, I would say, *consists in the power, which the members of the state reserve to themselves, of arriving at the public offices; or at least, of having votes in the nomination of those who fill them*; and I would choose to call CIVIL LIBERTY *that power over their own actions, which the members of the state reserve to themselves, and which their offices must not infringe.*
An Essay on the First Principles of Government (1768).

Chance or Theory
More is owing to what we call chance, that is, philosophically speaking, to the observation of events arising from unknown causes, than to any proper design, or pre-conceived theory of the business.
Experiments and Observations of Different Types of Air (1774).

Science and Revolution
Works of fiction resemble those features which contrive to illustrate the principles of philosophy, such as globes and orreries, the use of which extend no further than the views of human ingenuity, whereas real history resembles experiments by the air pump, condensing engine and electrical machine which exhibit the operation of nature, and the God of nature himself. The English hierarchy (if there be anything unsound in its constitution)…has reason to tremble even at an air pump or electrical machine.
Experiments and Observations on Different Kinds of Air (1774).

Radical Criticism
Whatever will not bear the test of rigorous scrutiny must now be rejected….This will be the means of purging our religion from every thing that will not bear this rigorous examination; but it will contribute to the firmer establishment of everything that will bear it.
An History of the Corruptions of Christianity (1782).

Exploding the Political and Religious Establishment
We are, as it were, laying gunpowder, grain by grain, under the old building of error and superstition, which a single spark may hereafter inflame, so as to produce an instantaneous explosion: in consequence of which, that edifice, the erection of which has been the work of ages, may be overturned in a moment, and so effectually that the same foundation can never be built upon again.
Reflections on the Present State of Free Inquiry in this Country (1787).

History as Progress
A thousand circumstances shew how inferior the ancients were to the moderns in religious knowledge, in science in general, in government, in laws, both the laws of nations, and those of particular states, in arts, in commerce, in the conveniences of life in manners, and in consequence of all these in happiness.
Lectures on History and General Policy (1787).

Race and Religion
You will consider all mankind as brethren, and neighbours…As men, and as Christians…we should not rest ourselves not only for our relations…or friends; not

only for our countrymen; not only for Europeans, but for the different inhabitants of Asia, Africa or America; and not only for Christians but for Jews, Mahometans, and Infidels. And as we ought to feel for our fellow men we ought, to the utmost extent of our influence, to exert ourselves to relieve their distresses.
A Sermon on the Subject of the Slave Trade…(1788).

The Purpose of Education
Train our youth to the new light which is now almost everywhere bursting out in favour of the civil rights of men…let every young mind expand itself, catch the rising gale, and partake of the glorious enthusiasm, the great objects of which are the flourishing state of science, arts, manufactures, and commerce, the extinction of wars, with the calamities incident to mankind for them, the abolishing of all useless distinctions, which were the offspring of a barbarous age.
Proper Objects of Education in the Present State of the World (1791).

Tablet dedicated to Joseph Priestley in the Church of the Messiah Broad Street. The tablet is now in the Unitarian Church, Ladywood, Birmingham. Local Studies and History, Birmingham Central Library.

Chapter 14

ENLIGHTENMENT AND DISSENT – A POEM

Roi Kwabena

This poem was commissioned by the Revolutionary Players Project to commemorate the 200th anniversary of the death of Joseph Priestley on 6th February 2004. It was performed at the launch of the Revolutionary Players website at Austin Court, Birmingham on 17th February 2004. The poem is located on www.revolutionaryplayers.org.uk and is reproduced here by kind permission of the author.

nullo discrimine
nullo discrimine
nullo discrimine

recent ancestors
have enjoyed carbonated beverages
soda water for flatulence
tonic water for the gin
rum and cola wars still pervade

moments of silence… rather reflection
will fill this poem
in humility to the all
as priestley would prefer
as we yet in our current mad haste
traditionally post modernist
to redress, reinterpret, revise
re-invent the now rusted wheel
as it is ……… (silence)

let us celebrate
this legacy

as we gather in Birmingham
city of trades

where industry married art
bearing prosperity

this revolutionary one
was here ... for many moons

(silence)

for enlightenment and dissent
reviled
exiled
his works publicly burnt
the mob relentless
destroyed his places of worship and work,
even his home

hounded by the press
of London
caricatured as the Priestley politician
or the political priest

his ideas are still ahead of our time

scientific pursuits for useless wars we still toil
terror occupies the survival space
of so many
this is how we use chemistry
have we learnt any lessons
1773-2004

cities besieged...nations in turmoil
disorder hunger an' disease

ancestor Priestley once you too
with your family were refugees to America
as many today to the north from the south the east and west
in search of a utopian sanctuary

their homes and families rent asunder
innocence maimed, dismembered
sacred trusts trampled by religious bigotry

electricity is not global
but a commodity to the highest bidder
science is viewed in many quarters
with not covert suspicion

we still ferry as in
horse-drawn fly boats
corroded dreams along silent canals
discarded machines survive as forgotten ghosts
in the glare of neon lights

still empty warehouses
an overgrown silence
inviting vandals and addicts
productivity replaced by determined vandalism

for carbon monoxide reigns predominant now
forget the love of liberty
being a Jacobean
look today at Haiti
from where else America sourced the guns
just like those manufactured in Birmingham
to fight numerous wars an' revolutions

but still the resilient Priestley advises
restraint, tolerance in spite
of adversity,
temperance
understanding for the originators of civilisation
the fathers and mothers of the once wretched slaves
for they too are humans
hence his work on the history of the corruption of Christianity

is this humanity's fate
should we like that mob who burnt his book
prod along as the old Birmingham

groping in the shadow of Soho house
neglecting lessons of the past
on a full moon
as the gun revisits us in Aston
forgive galton
we still eat chocolate
drink coffee, smoke tobacco
fair traded or not
we, especially those of us who can afford it
even contribute our daily share of carbon monoxide

even our love for vegetation has waned
yet priestley promised us a window in this crisis
with suitable humility the success we so crave
can be attained
reconnecting us to
a calm that we have long forgotten

flowers still bloom, hybrid or genetically modified
preachers and politicians still bray
as an intelligent young girl of 12 from Handsworth,
whose parents hail from Leeds,
visits the Science museum
dreaming to be a nuclear physicist.

CONTRIBUTORS

Patrick Baird
Patrick Baird is Joint Head of Local Studies and History Service at Birmingham Central Library. He was born in Birmingham and educated at St Philip's Grammar School, Edgbaston. Patrick is a founder member of the Birmingham and District Local History Association and has been its secretary since its formation. He is also President of both the Small Heath and East Birmingham Local History Societies. He has contributed to a number of books and journals dealing with local history, and his latest book is *The Bull Ring* (2004).

Dr Malcolm Dick
Malcolm Dick is Lecturer in Lifelong Learning at the University of Birmingham and Manager of the Joseph Priestley and Birmingham Project. Between 2000 and 2002 he was Editor and then Director of the Millennibrum Project and from 2002 to 2004 Manager of the Revolutionary Players Digitisation Project. His research interests include the Lunar Society and history of Birmingham and his latest publications include a history of refugees in Birmingham and contributions to books on migration and Englishness. He is completing two books on the city's history.

Gay Hill
Now a family and local history lecturer, mostly for the Workers Educational Association, Gay Hill worked at Sandwell Community History and Archives Service and as a Visiting Lecturer for the University of Birmingham. She has also contributed to the Revolutionary Players website. Gay is especially interested in non-conformist history and has completed a special study of early Quakerism in Birmingham and Aston.

Professor Peter Jones
Peter Jones is Professor of French History at the University of Birmingham, United Kingdom. He carried out research in the field of French rural history (18th and 19th centuries) for many years, but recently switched his interests to the cultural history of science. At present he is working on a project to explore the scientific and technological Enlightenment in the West Midlands, circa 1760-1820.

Dr Roi Ankhkara Kwabena
Roi was born in Trinidad. He is a cultural anthropologist whose creative work is commissioned by cultural, educational and local government agencies across the

world. Currently Vice-Chair of Birmingham Partnership against Racial Harassment, he was recently appointed the European Representative for the International Alliance Against Racism Xenophobia & Related Intolerance. This UNCHR registered NGO is charged with the responsibility of seeking reparations for human rights violations. A published writer and historian, Roi was also Poet Laureate for Birmingham between 2001 and 2002. Dr Kwabena uses story-telling and critical analysis to examine the historical roots of racism and to assess the direct relevance this has on our lives.

Peter Leather

Peter Leather is the Lecturer in Birmingham Studies at the University of Birmingham and since 1988 has been writing a weekly column in *The Birmingham News* newspaper and its predecessors. He is the author of *A Brief History of Birmingham* and *The Buildings of Birmingham* as well as the chapter on "The Historic Environment: Archaeological Sites and Historic Buildings" in Carl Chinn's *Birmingham: Bibliography of a City*. He is also the Chair of the Birmingham & District Local History Association.

Shena Mason

Shena Mason was part of the Birmingham Museums and Art Gallery team on the restoration of Soho House, home of Joseph Priestley's friend Matthew Boulton. She has written a history of the Birmingham jewellery trade, and contributed to the Revolutionary Players website. She is currently working in the Archives of Soho at Birmingham City Archives, researching the life of Matthew Boulton's daughter.

Dr Goronwy Tudor Jones

Goronwy Tudor Jones is Reader in High Energy Physics at the University of Birmingham. He is a member of the Steering Committee of the CERN (European Centre for Particle Physics Research) High School Teachers Project and has for the last four years taught at the CERN HST Summer School. He is working with the novelist Alan Wall on a project funded by Arts Council England and the Arts and Humanities Research Board, aimed at bridging the gaps between the Arts and Sciences.

Dr Ruth Watts

Ruth Watts is Reader in History of Education at the University of Birmingham. Her teaching and research interests are in history of education, gender and cultural history and the teaching of history. Her publications include *Gender, Power and the Unitarians in England, 1760-1860*. The focus of her current research is on the cultural history of women and science. She is President of the History of Education Society and a member of the International Standing Conference for the History of Education (ISCHE) and the Women's History Network.

INDEX

Index Notes:

Page numbers printed in *italics* refer to illustrations within the text.

    Page numbers in roman numeral refer to pages of the picture gallery.

A

abolitionist campaign, 66–75
    and actions, 75–7
    slavery witnessed in America, 102
Acts of Parliament
    Blasphemy Act (1698), 25
    Occasional Conformity Act (1711), 26
    Reform Act (1832), 59
    Test and Corporation Acts, 14, 25–6, 28, 82
    Toleration Act (1689), 24–5
American Chemical Society, 108
Arianism, 10
Aris's Birmingham Gazette, 69, 73, 74, 83
Aristotle, 34
Armytage, Harry, 56
Artisans Library of Birmingham, 54

B

Baird, Patrick, 110, 121
Baskerville House, Birmingham, *85*
Batley grammar school, 8
Berington, Joseph, 65
Bird, Vivian, 81
Birmingham
    abolitionist campaign in, 67–77
    as industrial centre (1700s), 3, 12–13

    education provision (1700s-1800s), 53–60
    Priestley celebrations (2004), 3–4, 8, 117–20
    religious affiliations (1700s), 13–14
    Priestley's time at, 15, 27-9
    see also Priestley Riots
Birmingham and District Local History Association, 3
Birmingham and Midland Institute, 59
Birmingham Library, 27
    Priestley Collection, 110
Birmingham Museums and Art Gallery, 112
Black, Joseph, 39
Boulton, Matthew, 1, 22, 50, *76*
    and abolitionist campaign, 74, 75
Bowood House, Wiltshire, 3, 41–3
Boyle, Robert, 38
Brayley, Edward, 58
Brooke, John, 85, 86
Brotherly Society of Birmingham, 53–4, 55
Brownrigg, William, 39
Bruno, Giordano, 35
Burke, Edmund, *Reflections on the Revolution in France,* 15
Burn, Revd. Edward, 29
Byerley's school, Warwickshire, 60

C

Carles, Joseph, 85
Cavendish, Henry, 39, 42, 44–5
Church of England, 24–6
Clark, John Ruskin, 21

Clark, Thomas, 54
Clarkson, Thomas, 67, 74
Coleridge, Samuel Taylor, 10
Cook, Captain James, 38
Cooper, Thomas, 7, 106, 107, 108
Copernicus, 34
Copley Medal, 38
Coulomb, Charles Augustin de, 32, 35
Cowper, Martha, 60
Crowley, Ambrose, 26

D
Darwin, Erasmus, 1, 51, *52,* 52–3, 67
    abolitionist campaign and, 68
    Economy of Vegetation, The, 68
    Loves of the Plants, The, 68
Daventry Academy, 9–10, *10,* 31
Dawson, John, of Liverpool, 7575
Day, Thomas, 1, *51,* 67
    abolitionist campaign and, 67–8
    Dying Negro, The, 67–8
    Fragment of an original letter on the
        slavery of Negroes, 68
Dent, R K, *Old and New Birmingham,*
    81, *82*
Dick, Malcolm, 1, 5, 65, 105, 111, 114,
    121
Dissenters, 13–14, 23–5, 91
    civil liberties and, 23–5

E
Edgebaston High School for Girls, 60
Edgeworth, Maria, 50, 52, *53,* 56
Edgeworth, Richard Lovell, 1, 50, *50,*
    52
education
    Lunar Society and, 50–3
    Priestley's views on, 2, 19, 48–50, 116
    Unitarians and, 53–60
electricity, 36–7

Emans, Revd Mr., 69
Enlightenment, European, 2
Equiano, Olaudah, *73, 74*

F
Fair Hill, Priestley's Birmingham
    house, *84,* 86–7, *92,* 111–12
Female Society for the Relief of British
    Negro Slaves, 77
Fieldhead, Leeds, *9*
Finch, Catherine, 60
Finch, Sarah (daughter of JP), 17, 60
Fox, William, 74
Franklin, Benjamin, 40–1, 90
French Revolution, 2, 8, 17, 22–3, 76, 82
    Paris, post-Robespierre, 95–6
    viewed by Dissenters, 14, 91

G
Galileo, 34, 38
"Gallic Commemoration Dinner" (14th
    July 1791), 83–5, 91, VII
Galton, Mary Anne *see*
    Schimmelpenninck, Mary Anne
Galton, Samuel, 74, 75, 76
Galton, Samuel (junior), 1, 53, *54*
    and abolitionist campaign, 67, 76
Garbett, Samuel, 74
gaseous chemistry, 11, 37–41
Gibbs, F.W., 28, 32, 34, 43
Gillray, James "*A Birmingham Toast,*
    July 14th, 1791", 82
Great Book of Sufferings, 25
Greek natural philosophy, 34–5
Guericke, Otto von, 38

H
handbills and pamphlets, 11, 32, 73, 84
Hartley, David, 33
    Observations on Man, 48

Hazelwood school, Birmingham, 56–8
Hill family, 56–9
Hill, Gay, 21, 121
Hill, Thomas Wright, 55–6
Hill-Top school, Birmingham, 56, 60
Horsley, Bishop Samuel, *25*
Hutton, Catherine, on JP, 21, 22
Hutton, Thomas, 85
Hutton, William, 15
    on JP, 21–2, 24
    Priestley Riots and, 81

J
Jefferson, Thomas, 107, 108
Jones, David, 54
Jones, Dr Goronwy Tudor, 31, 122
Jones, Professor P. M., 7, 111, 121
Joseph Priestley House Museum, 108,
    112

K
Keir, James, 1, 82
Kwabena, Dr Roi Ankhkara, 117,
    121–2

L
Langford, J. A., *A Century of*
    Birmingham Life, 67
Langford, Paul, 24
Lavoisier, Antoine, 11–12, *12,* 20,
    41–3, 45
Leather, Peter, 81, 122
Leigh Smith, Barbara, 60
Lindsay, Jack, 33
Lindsey, Revd Theophilus, 12, *13,* 18, 20
Lloyd, Charles, 74
Lloyd, Sampson, 26
Locke, John, 48
London, 16–17
Luckcock, James, 55

Lunar Society, 16, 43, 50–3
    and abolitionist campaign, 67–8,
        74–6
    as educative, 50–3
    members of, 1, 21, 22

M
Madan, Spencer, 15, 23, 26
Mansfield, Lord, 67
Martineau, Martin, 81, 84, 85
Mason, Shena, 90, 122
Matthews, William, 53–4
Methodism, 23–4
Middletown, Connecticut, *VIII,* 99–100,
    100, 101–2
Mill Hill Chapel, Leeds, 10, 11
Money, John, 27, 33

N
Nantwich, Cheshire, 10, 31
Needham Market, Suffolk, 10, 31
New Meeting House, Birmingham, *2,*
    3, *3,* 8, 12, *15,* 55
    during riots, *83,* 86
    educational activities, 53–5
New York City (1768), *94*
nitric oxide, 39–40
Northumberland, Pennsylvania, *VIII,*
    19, 98–9, 101, 105–8
Nott, John, 23

O
Osler, Follet, 58–9
oxygen, discovery of, 12, 41–2

P
Paine, Thomas, *IV,* 17
pamphlets and handbills, 11, 32, 73, 84
Paris, the Russell family's visit, 95–6
Parkes, Bessie, 60

Pemberton, Josiah, 54
Perrott, Francis, 74
Philadelphia, Pennsylvania, 98, 99,
    105, 107
phlogiston theory, 18, 41–2
Pitt, William, 27, 77
political repression, 2–3
Poor Laws, 3, 23
Porter, Roy, 24
Presbyterians, 23
Price, Dr Richard, 12
Priestley, Henry (son of JP), 17, 107
Priestley, Joseph
    as abolitionist, 65, 67, 68–73, 74, 77,
        107
    character, 8, 15, 21–2, 27, 29, 110–1
    early career, 10–11, 31
    as educationalist, 2, 19, 48–50, 116
        Lunar Society and, 50–3
    intellectual contribution, 1, 18–19
    life events
        chronology of, 5-6
        birth, 1, 8
        marriage, 11
        death of wife and son, 101, 107
        death, 1, 7–8, 107–8
    life in America, 17–18, 105–8
        Russell family's visit, 94, 99–101
    life in Birmingham, 90
        as minister, 15
        controversy at Library, 27
        earns nickname "Gunpowder Joe,"
            27–9
        involvement in riots, 19, 22, 34,
            81–7, 91–2
    life in London, 16-17
    political views, 1, 114
        controversy concerning, 107
        on poverty and punishment, 23
        on religious freedoms, 26–7

religious beliefs
    as a young man, 1–2, 9–10, 11, 12
    faces opposition to, 23-7
    and metaphysics, 32, 33–4
scientific experiments, 11
    in electricity, 36–7
    in gases, 11, 37–41
    oxygen, discovery of, 12, 41–2
    in respiration, 43, 45
    synthesis of water, 43–5
works
    *Appeal to the Professors of
        Christianity,* 24
    Case for Poor Emigrants, 106
    Chart of Biography, 32
    *Essays on the First Principles of
        Government,* 22, 114
    Evidences of Revelation, 100
    *Experiments and Observations on
        Different Kinds of Air,* 38,
        115
    Familiar Letters II, 27
    Familiar Letters III, 28–9
    Familiar Letters XI, 21
    *History and Present State of
        Electricity,* 11, 36
    History of the Christian Church,
        106
    *History of the Corruptions of
        Christianity, An,* 27, 115
    housed at Birmingham Central
        Library, 110
    *Lectures on History and General
        Policy,* 115
    *Letters to the Inhabitants of
        Northumberland,* 107
    *Observations on Different Kinds
        of Air,* 35
    *Observations on Respiration and
        the Use of Blood,* 43

Reflections on the Present state of Free Inquiry in this Country, 27
Rudiments of English Grammar, 32
Sermon on the Subject of the Slave Trade, A, 69–73, *110,* 116
Theory of Language, and Universal Grammar, The, 32
bibliography of works on, 111–13
Priestley, Joseph (son of JP), 7, 17, 98, 107–8
Priestley, Mary (wife of JP), *I,* 8, 16, 107, 112
Priestley, William (son of JP), 17
Priestley celebrations, Birmingham (2004), 3-4, 8, 117-20
Priestley Collection, Birmingham, 110
Priestley Riots, Birmingham (1791), 12, 16, 34, 81–7, 91–2
    events leading up to, 19, 21–3, 31–15
    see also Birmingham

Q
Quakers, 16, 24–5
    abolitionist campaign and, 67, 72, 76

R
Rees, Abraham
    Chemistry Laboratory, 38
    Electrical Machines, 36
religion and science, 11
religious pluralism, 9–10
Repeal of the Test Act: A Vision, 28
respiratory science, 43, 45
Revolutionary Players Project, 117
riots of 1791 *see* Priestley Riots
Rose, R B, 81, 82
Royal Society, 11, 16, 36, 38
Russell, Martha, diary of, 94–5, 96, 97, 98
    marriage, 102–3

Russell, Mary, diary of, 96, 98–9, 101–2
    painting of Middletown, *VIII*
Russell, Thomas, diary of, 97, 98, 99–100
Russell, William, and family, 74, *83,* 87, 90–1, *91*
    Priestley Riots and, *86,* 92–3
    journey to America, 94–8
    life in America, 98–103
Rutt, John Towill, 27
Ryland, Thomas, 55, 60, *85*

S
Schimmelpenninck, Mary Anne, 77
    on JP, 21
    on slave trade, 74–5
science and religion, 11
scientific experiment, development of, 35–6
scientific experiments of Joseph Priestley
    in electricity, 36–7
    in gases, 11, 37–41
    oxygen, discovery of, 12, 41–2
    in respiration, 43, 45
    synthesis of water, 43–5
Shelburne, Earl of, 11, *11,* 12
Skey, James, 102–3, *103*
slavery *see* abolitionist campaign
Small, William, 1, 107
Smith, Barbara M D, 76
Smith, Martin, 22, 29
Soho House, Birmingham, 45
St Michael's Catholic Church *see* New Meeting House
St Philip's Church, Birmingham, *26*
Sturge, Joseph, 77
sugar trade and slavery, 74–5
synthesis of water, 43–5

T

Timmins Collection, 111
    A Philosopher, III
    Death and Pain and P.....y, The, IV
    Friends of the People, The, VI
    Magnetic Dispensary, III
    Mr Burke's pair of Spectacles, V
    Political Portraiture, II
    *Treacherous Rebel and Birmingham
        Rioter, The*, IV
Torricelli, Evangelista, 38

U

Uglow, Jenny, 67
Unitarianism, 10, 12, 15, 24, 33
    Blasphemy Act (1698) and, 25
    education and, 53–60
University of Birmingham, 59, 111
Upton, Chris, 81

V

Villiers, William, 74
Voltaire, 9

W

Walker, Zacheus, 103
war between Britain and France (1793),
    17, 77
Warrington, 31, 37–41
Warrington Academy, 10
Warwickshire Constitutional Society, 22
water, synthesis of, 43–4
Watt, James, 1, 8, 22, *23*, 44–5
    and abolitionist campaign, 75
Watts, Dr Ruth, 48, 122
Wedgwood, Josiah, 1, 51, 52, *66*, 67
    abolitionist campaign and, 68
Wesley, John, 23, *24*
*Westley's East Prospect of
    Birmingham, 14*

Whitehurst, John, 1
Wilberforce, William, 74
Wilkinson, John, 16, 90
Wilkinson, Mary, *see* Priestley, Mary
Withering, William, 1
Wollstonecraft, Mary, 96, 97
women
    and abolitionist campaign, 77
    education, 52–3, 54, 59–60

Y

Young, Arthur, 13